Mighty in the Land

Raising powerful children for God

Julia O'Mahony

Unless otherwise indicated,
all scripture quotations are taken from the
New King James Version of the Bible.

Other scripture quotations taken from the Holy Bible,
New International Version copyright ©1973, 1978, 1984
International Bible Society.
Used with permission.

Mighty in the Land
ISBN 0-9540268-0-2
Copyright © 2001 by Julia O'Mahony

Published by O'Mahony Ministries
P.O. Box 4,
Greystones, Co. Wicklow,

Cover Design by Ann O'Mahony
Printed in the Republic of Ireland.

All rights reserved under International Copyright Law.
Contents and/or cover may not be reproduced in whole or
in part in any form without the express written consent of the Publisher.

CONTENTS

1. God's Vision for your Children 1
2. Training and Character 12
3. Attitude, Attitude, Attitude 20
4. Discipline and Deliver 30
5. Love and Encouragement 38
6. Good-Bye Mr. Average 46
7. Don't be Afraid to say "NO" 50
8. Joyful Sounds 56
9. The Power of your Confession 61
10. Your Prayers make Dynamite Available 70
11. Holy Spirit Wisdom 76
12. Building Close Relationships 81
13. The Limits are Off 90
14. Rewards of your Labour 94
    Prayer for Salvation 98
    Confessions of a Parent 99

ACKNOWLEDGMENTS

Sean, thank you for all the support and encouragement you gave me while I put my thoughts into writing. You have always encouraged me and never held me back, and for that I am so grateful.

Mark, Rebecca, April and Debbie, I'm so blessed to have you as my kids! I always say that I am glad that God sent you to live in my house. Rebecca, thank you for the many hours of work you put in during the summer of 2000. Also to you Mark, it has been great working alongside you. It has been a wonderful adventure being parents to the four of you. You are truly mighty in the land.

My parents, Henry and Stella Clarke, who although no longer with us, instilled many Godly principles into my life, in spite of the fact that they didn't have the privilege of being taught the Word of God in the same depth as myself. I owe so much to them and take this opportunity to honour them both.

Frank Cairns, you inspired and motivated me to get this book into print. Your enthusiasm moved me into action. You and your precious wife, Sylvia are very special to us.

Ann O'Mahony, your work on this project has been deeply appreciated. Both your time and your helpful advice have been a great bonus to us. It's been a pleasure to work with you. Thank you for being so willing.

Sara Thomas, you are such a blessing and have a wonderful gift with your camera. Bless you for being willing to help us.

Pastors Mark and Jacque Putnam, and the people of Victory Christian Church in Colombia, Missouri who supported the publishing of this book, and believed in us. We deeply appreciate your help and have been so blessed by your friendship.

And to you Lord God, who has given us the principles in your Word to teach and train our children. You are the reason I have written this book. May your people truly love you and be committed to raising the next generation to be Mighty in the Land.

ENDORSEMENTS

This book was birthed out of a search for Bible-based instruction for Julia's own family and a deep desire to see the parents of the next generation equipped to have God's will established in the hearts of their children. Julia's vision for the family, combined with her knowledge of the scriptures and personal experiences has earned her the right to produce such a work as this. This book will inspire and give godly wisdom to the parents of the next generation.

In a society where moral standards are falling and divorce rate is on the increase, a book like this is needed. It will challenge the parents to become leaders of their family and instruct them how to rise out of the status quo to become all that God has declared they can be.

Pastor Joe Corry: Founder and Pastor of Craigavon Pentecostal Church, Lakeland Pentecostal Church and Destiny International Broadcasters, Northern Ireland.

The publication of this book is timely, coming as it does when respect for the sanctity of marriage is in decline, single motherhood is increasing at an alarming rate and family life is morally threatened. Authoress Julia O'Mahony writes from the experiences of her childhood years. The autobiographical details are profound. They led her to identify the satanic enemy as merciless. She did not find the answers in dead religion, but in Jesus. This book will be of great benefit to parents in the raising of their children.

Pastor Sheila Hade, Victory Christian Centre, Dublin, Ireland.

FOREWORD

I know that like me you want the best for your children - and you expect the best from your children. The incredible promise of the Saviour is this: "If ye abide in me, and my words abide in you, ye shall ask what ye will, and it shall be done unto you" (John 15:7). You can have what you ask.

Now here are the questions: "What are you asking for, and what are you believing God for, in the lives of your children?" This powerful new book by Julia O'Mahony will show you how to ask for and raise children who will not just be good - they'll be mighty in the land.

Julia speaks from the firm granite of settled experience. She and her husband have wonderful children who are mighty for God. They are as well-known for the love and cohesion of their family as they are for the thoughtfulness and power of their teaching. This book is a must read for every parent. I recommend it highly.

Walter Hallam: Pastor and founder of Abundant Life Christian Center and Abundant Life Ministries of National Destiny, Texas, USA.

INTRODUCTION

There are many instructions and promises in the Scriptures concerning our children. There are however still many Christians who have suffered needlessly because of a lack of knowledge of God's will for their children and His ways in their upbringing. It is sad to see people raised in Christian homes where parents know and serve the Lord and yet the children have no interest in God. They grow up with an indifferent attitude to the things of God preferring to be anywhere else but in Church. It is not God's will that parents raise children who rebel against Him.

As I studied the scriptures, I found God's vision for our children was far bigger than I had first anticipated. His heart is for our descendants to be full of the Holy Spirit, powerful and effective in the earth.

As Christians we may be confident to say, "I am saved, I am born again, my sin is forgiven and heaven is my home." But we are probably not so confident to say, "My children will be mighty in the land, they will be taught by the Lord and great shall be their peace."

Parents need to be confident in the Word of God concerning their children and convinced of His will. God's ways and thoughts need to become more important to us than tradition, circumstances and the opinion of others.

Whatever situation you are in right now, God wants to show himself strong on your behalf. He wants to enable you to raise a family that is mighty in the land. It is my prayer that you will take God's word and apply it to your own life, allowing it to instruct and direct you. With His Word in your heart and by yielding to the direction of the Holy Spirit you can raise your children to be all that God intended for them to be.

CHAPTER ONE

GOD'S VISION FOR YOUR CHILDREN

MY SEARCH

Before I ever had children of my own I began to read, study and look for all the help I could get on raising a family. You see I was desperate to find God's way and determined that my children would never have to be exposed to the situations that I faced while growing up. My search opened up for me the promises of God that I had no idea were available all along for His people. It has been discovery after discovery of the wonderful future and plans God has for our children. Alongside finding His plan I have had to learn what my responsibility is in this. For as a parent I have an incredible opportunity to shape lives of the next generation. Those lives will have an impact on others, whether good or bad. It is more far reaching than just my family and I. It never stops just there. But every parent is raising someone who will impart to others, someone who has unlimited potential on the inside of them. Let me open up my own life and share with you what led me to this search.

I had been bought up in a good home. My parents were extremely hard working. My mother worked tirelessly in the house, as well as helping my father with his business. He was a builder. I often admired the homes he had built in the surrounding villages. When I rode to school on the bus I would frequently see a sign, "H.T. Clarke Builders" and I would think quietly to myself, "That's my dad."

We had a good home that he had worked on and extended. It seemed that every vegetable that I could name was grown in our large garden. June and July was fruit picking time, and I would enjoy gathering baskets of raspberries, strawberries, blackcurrants and gooseberries. In the cooler month of September it was time to pick apples. I would be sent armed with cardboard boxes to collect and carefully store the apples that would be used in the winter months. I loved climbing to the end of those branches and reaching for the fruit that would be furthest away, wondering if I would be able to retrieve them without knocking them to the ground first. Then there were the pears, plums and greengages to be gathered.

The field at the back of our home belonged to my father where I spent many summer days playing with cousins and friends. I knew all the best places to find birds nests, and would watch from a distance until the eggs had hatched and the young had flown. Finding frogspawn was like finding a valuable treasure to me. I would bring some home and put it in an old tin bath and watch those tadpoles develop into tiny frogs. It seemed an idyllic life and a carefree way to spend my childhood.

We belonged to the local church where my father was the churchwarden and as far as I remember, my parents never missed a service. When I was about twelve or thirteen years old a missionary family came to live in our village. They started a Bible study, which I attended along with one or two others. Sometimes I was the only one. Every Sunday morning I walked a mile to the Old Rectory dining room and would sit around that huge polished table smelling the homely aroma of coffee and toast, while hearing the gospel of how God so loved the world that He gave Jesus to die for us. I had never heard anything like it before. I had attended church and Sunday school all my life but had never heard that God loved me. Maybe I had not been listening, or maybe it had not been preached. It seemed the easiest decision in the world to make Jesus the Lord of my life after hearing how much he had done for me. Those times around the Bible in that rectory home back in 1967 were the beginning of my walk with God and a hunger to know more about the One who had given His life for me.

Soon after that the situation in our home began to change. My older brother became ill with what the doctors termed depression and schizophrenia. There began endless hospital visits. Then followed suicide attempts and sometimes, uncontrolled violence. It seemed I was in the middle of this from a young age, not knowing how to handle it, and at many times trying to protect my parents. People were kind and wanted to help but no one seemed to have any answers. The doctors would prescribe drugs that would suppress things for a short while, but there was no lasting help. The church we were in was sympathetic but did not know how to help. And yet I had read in the Bible how Jesus set people free and gave them their right mind. I knew there was an answer somewhere. But where could I find others to help me bring that answer into reality.

As my parents grew into old age they became more distraught, blaming themselves for what had happened in their family, and not knowing how to bring about a change for the better. In 1987 my father eventually could bare it no longer and took an overdose of sleeping tablets to end his life. He was following on the footsteps of his older brother who had gassed himself in his car just a few years before, unable to cope with life. Shortly after that my two first cousins took their lives.

So I began to make a more determined decision that this would not come on my children. I was now married and living in Ireland away form the English countryside where I had grown up and away from my family. I was discovering from the Word of God that Jesus sets people free, breaks curses and brings abundant life and restoration into lives. I searched to find God's will. I knew that he was a good God whose overwhelming love caused Him to send His own Son to die for mankind. I made another quality decision that I would never bring my children into dead religion that has no real answers for real people.

You see the devil comes to kill, steal and destroy lives. He has no mercy. The Bible says that through lack of knowledge we perish. We had been a family perishing in a sea of hopelessness because we had no knowledge of the truth of the healing and deliverance that God had made available to us.

But the Bible also says that if you seek him with all your heart you will find Him. So I began to search for answers on how to bring up my children in a safe, peaceful, secure environment. It has been a wonderful search. I have discovered far more of the riches of God's goodness and vision for our children than I had first anticipated.

Like Joseph, situations came into my life at a young age, that were meant for evil but God has turned them for good. I believe with all my heart that the truths you find in these pages will cause you to raise mighty powerful children if you will take them and run with them as I have. They will bring about tremendous change not just in the lives of individual families but will have an effect of imparting to many others also.

GOD'S VISION FOR OUR CHILDREN

Every parent knows that after the excitement of their newborn's arrival there is a lot of hard work, discipline, fun and tears involved. The Word of God paints a picture of God's plan for our children. His will is good, pleasing and perfect. So as you follow His guidelines you can expect the best for your child. So we need to look at His promises to see what we are aiming for, to see our destination. Later we will look at how to reach it.

"For I will pour water on Him who is thirsty, and floods on

> **the dry ground; I will pour My Spirit on your descendants, and my blessing on your offspring; they will spring up among the grass like willows by the watercourses. One will say I am the Lord's another will call Himself by the name of Jacob; another will write with His hand, "The Lord's," and name Himself by the name of Israel." Isaiah 44:3-5**

What a beautiful promise. If I am thirsty for the things of God, He will pour out on my life and not just on my life but on the lives of my children. It doesn't matter how dry or difficult my situation is, God says if I get thirsty for Him he will pour out His Holy Spirit on me and His blessing on my children. What parent does not wish to see their child blessed, protected, safe from harm and mentally and physically strong. It is God's desire to pour out His blessing, His goodness, His favour and preferential treatment on our children to increase them exceedingly. We are given these promises so that we can know God's will and act in faith on His Word. His desire and purpose for our children is for them to grow up strong in the Lord, mature, full of the Holy Spirit, unashamedly declaring the things of God. Each child being the unique individual God has made them, using the various gifts and talents that they have, and walking in the abundance and blessing that God has for them.

> **"For you shall expand to the right and to the left, and your descendants will inherit the nations, and make the desolate cities inhabited." Isaiah 54:3**

This verse tells us that our children will affect cities and nations. I believe God's vision for our children is far more powerful and far-reaching than we would ever dare to dream or imagine. This verse takes us far beyond just my little family and I. God thinks big. He thinks cities and nations. He thinks effectiveness and exceedingly fruitful. As I examine this verse I realise how important it is to take raising children seriously. To get rid of small-mindedness and self-centredness and get into God's idea of raising children who have a strong spirit of faith so that they can accomplish all that God has intended for them. For this verse tells us that God has others in mind when we raise our children. The cities and nations of the earth are on His heart. The Earth belongs to God but has been in the hands of the enemy of mankind. He is looking to our descendants and declaring you are going to get it back. You are going to affect cities and nations. As I have meditated on this scripture I realise there is no place for small thinking and low living when we raise our children. There is no room for half-heartedness and compromise. God's vision for our children is far greater than we can imagine and as parents we need to consider very carefully our responsibilities as we raise them.

As we examine Isaiah 54:13, we see God's will for our children to be taught by the Lord. It is our responsibility to see that we teach them the things of God and bring them to church where they can experience the power of God and where they are taught His Word. Then we can expect the fruit of great peace in their lives. Peace is wonderful in our lives and in the lives of our children, nothing missing in their lives, nothing broken or spoilt but God's abundant peace in their hearts and minds. Peace of mind is available for our children in a world of confusion and distress as they are taught of the Lord. In order for our children to be taught by the Lord they need to have a hearing heart, and a desire for the things of God and a listening ear. As parents we need to teach and show them the wonderful goodness of God, so that desire and hunger can grow and develop. They are growing up in a world where people are unaware of the goodness of God. When our children begin to experience this for themselves it builds a confidence in their hearts towards God and his willingness to be good to them. As they come to know God for themselves they will learn to hear from God, they will be taught by the Lord, guided and directed as they grow older and able to hear His voice for themselves.

SONS AND DAUGHTERS

Psalms 144:12 describes how our sons may be as plants grown up in their youth, tender at first, and vulnerable, but growing stronger as parents watch over them. Parents must take their responsibility to make sure that they are trained and nurtured until they are strong and mature enough to handle their lives with wisdom. Psalms 1 tells us how blessed a young man like this is. He becomes strong like a tree that grows beside water. His life is fruitful. Whatever he puts his hand to, will prosper because he delights to follow God's ways, therefore supernatural favour and blessing is upon his life. Who in their right mind would not want to see their sons growing up like this?

Our daughters will also be strong, according to this Psalm, immovable and focused, like sculptured pillars in a palace. They will have a purity and dignity about them, stable and not easily moved by others. In other words, not bowing to peer pressure, but completely established in the ways of God, rooted and fixed. A palace speaks of a place of dignity and majesty, if they are to be like sculptured pillars they will be fitting for a king, dressing and behaving in a manner that will honour the King of all Kings.

We see from all these scriptures a wonderful picture emerging of God's plan or, as I like to call it, God's dream, for our children. Don't ever give up on your children. Don't give up on the fight of faith, you do your part and let God do His. He won't disappoint you. For He is able to do exceeding abundantly above all that you could ask or think.

According to Joel 2:28-29 our sons and daughters will prophesy, so we can expect the prophetic from them as they grow. We need to encourage them and pray with them at home. Encourage them to pray over family members, sharing scriptures and encouraging them to minister to one another. As they grow older it will be natural for them to hear from God, prophesy and bring a Word from God that will change someone's life forever.

Joel 2:28 also tells us that our sons shall see visions, so expect your sons to develop a keen awareness to the things of the Spirit, being led by the Spirit and having the Holy Spirit on them in a powerful way.

These are just some of the promises God has for our children, painting a beautiful picture of strength, peacefulness and a close walk with God, enabling them to do great things in the Kingdom of God. This is something all born again, spirit-filled parents should desire for their children, and it is possible, because all things are possible to Him who believes.

But how do we get there? How do we arrive at this destination, when all around us seem to be going in the opposite direction? God has promised us everything for life and godliness, through our knowledge of Him. 2 Peter 1:3.

So you are equipped with everything you need to raise a powerful family. The conditions are to obey Him, do and say things His way, one day at a time.

If your children are away from God then Jeremiah 31:16-17 tells you to stop crying and being upset about them, your work will be rewarded, they shall come back from the land of the enemy. Start doing some work that can be rewarded by God. Begin by thanking Him that they are coming back from the land of the enemy. They are coming off drugs, out of alcoholism or rebellion in the name of Jesus or whatever other situation you need to believe for them. Believe God's promise, have it firmly implanted in your heart. Meditate on it until you are convinced of it. Speak it out over them. Expect nothing less until you see it come to pass. Never speak doubt or unbelief concerning the promise of God. Stay focused and you will see your answer.

Parents you play such an important part in moulding and shaping your children's character and therefore their future. Mothers in particular have tremendous influence in instilling Godly principles and Godly attitudes into children's lives.

It is so important not to be over busy or preoccupied so you can be sensitive when one of your children needs time and attention. Or when you maybe need to seek God for wisdom about handling some situation on their behalf. If we are too busy or distracted we may miss the problem with which God wanted us to deal. So the key is to find out God's will for our children and then establish our responsibility in parenting.

MIGHTY IN THE LAND

"Praise the Lord. Blessed is the man who fears the Lord, who finds great delight in His commands. His children will be mighty in the land; the generation of the upright will be blessed." Psalm 112:1-2 NIV

God has given us tremendous keys in training up children. But this is not for the casual listener. It is for the one who will GREATLY delight in His command. It is for the parent who will quickly obey God and enjoy putting His ways first in every area. It takes time for us to renew our mind to the things of God. It is a process. It takes a conscious decision of our will not to be conformed to the pattern of this world, (Rom 12:2) but to be transformed by the renewing of your mind. When we do that, we are able to prove what is the good, pleasing and perfect will of God.

DELIGHT GREATLY

To delight greatly in something means to take pleasure in and to cherish. It is something that becomes attractive to us. In this scripture, a blessed person is one who finds God's commandments attractive, and desirable. So much so that they will put aside other things of less importance in order to pursue them. They become a priority as Matthew 6:33 says, and as they begin to give them first place the blessings of God start to overtake them.

Ask yourself, "Are the ways of God intensely attractive to me?" If not, repent and start worshipping and praising God, spending time in His presence until your heart is affectionate towards Him. Allow Him to show you where you have been cold, or lukewarm, and make a QUALITY decision to turn from that. If you do you part, God will do His, and your heart will be warmed to Him, your spirit trusting Him again. This in turn will affect your children, whom God desires to become mighty.

If we want this promise to become a reality in our lives, then we have to do our part. The promise is not just for anyone. It does not say for the churchgoer, for the Christian, for the one who does the most work in the ministry. All those maybe good but the promise is for the one who greatly delights in God's ways. Let's remind ourselves, God means what He says, and says what He means.

ANCHOR YOURSELF

Quality decisions are so important in our walk with God and in bringing up children. When we decide to do things God's way we are going against the "norm". That's why we need to have God's Word fixed in our hearts. It will make us strong to do what is right instead of what everyone else expects. His Word acts like an anchor keeping us steady during difficult times.

There maybe times when you're tempted to think nothing is working. You may feel like giving up. But just like a tiny seed in the ground, nothing shows for a while but then, a tiny shoot appears. So you will discover tiny "shoots", little rays of hope, to encourage you and let you know this is working, keep going!

It is wonderful to know that God's ways work. They produce the results He promised. So when you anchor yourself in what he says, he will empower you to raise a family that will be blessed and be a blessing.

ANY OLD FISH

We can see from His Word that it is his will that our children grow to be mighty. Not just average, not easily intimidated. Not easily swayed by the opinions of others and following the crowd. I often tell my own children, "Any old fish can swim downstream, but it takes a fish with backbone to swim up stream."

Our children will get this "strong backbone" by their own walk with God. Knowing Him, spending time with Him, enjoying His presence will give them a taste for the things of God. Seeing that His ways work will cause a desire to follow Him and hear His voice for themselves. They will become confident in His goodness and blessing towards them. This in turn will cause them to be able to "swim up stream," against society and peer pressures, because they know that they know that the word of God works, and it is working for them.

CHAPTER TWO

TRAINING AND CHARACTER

"Hear, my children the instruction of a father. And give attention to understanding. For I give you good doctrine: Do not forsake my law. When I was my father's son. Tender and the only one in the sight of my mother. He also taught me, and said to me: Let your heart retain my words; Keep my commands, and live."
Proverbs 4:1-4

God holds parents responsible for the upbringing of their children, not schools, youth leaders or churches. Although each of these groups may influence a child, the final responsibility is with the parents. In order to train children properly they should be surrounded by an atmosphere of encouragement, security and love.

The scripture in Proverbs 4:1-4 shows that parents are to take the time to instruct their children. There were lessons and instructions from the parents that would be so vital in the lives of their children that they would need to pay close attention to and make sure that they did not forget. This training from their parents could actually be a matter of life or death to their children. This reminds me that it is not only the training that is the responsibility of the parent, but also to make sure the child understands and puts into practice what has been taught. Parents have a responsibility to know how their children are behaving when they are not around.

BE DILIGENT

Deuteronomy 6:6 "And these words which I command you today shall be in your heart. You shall teach DILIGENTLY to your children, and shall talk of them when you sit in your house, when you walk by the way, when you lie down, and when you rise up."

I love that word 'diligently'! God loves diligence. It means getting rid of being half-hearted and taking seriously what He requires of us as parents. It means that God's ways have to first of all be in my heart. I have to be living it out in my life and then teaching it to my children. Your children should be able to see that everything you teach them you are walking in yourself. This means parents need to make sure they are nor over busy but make the time and deliberately teach their children. One of the hazards today in parenting is that parents can be so busy, with both working in many cases, they are not always aware of the needs that should be dealt with. Being too tired to take their responsibility small issues can soon grow and before long seeds of bitterness and rebellion can grow in the heart of a child towards the parent and therefore towards the words the parents speaks to them. When parents notice children becoming withdrawn and sullen it is time to spend some quality time with them. It is not a time to become more preoccupied with their own agendas.

God expects that parents spend time with their children at home, when their out walking or more appropriately for us when we are in the car. Also, going to bed and getting up. That's just about all the time! God seems to have covered every part of life and is saying, "Parents, I'm expecting you to communicate, teach and train your children. This training should be both practical and spiritual. Teaching both how to look after themselves and their possessions plus how to treat other people. Spiritually they need to learn of the goodness of God and the blessing of following His ways.

TRAINING

"Train up a child in the way he should go, and when he is old he will not depart from it." Proverbs 22:6

Children need to be trained in the ways of God, in other words they need to be given a "taste" of the goodness of God. Psalm 34:8 says, "Oh, taste see that the Lord is good, Blessed is the man who trusts in Him". When they know that He loves and cares for them, that He blesses and protects them, this will give them a taste to want to serve Him.

They should be trained according to their gifts and personalities. They need opportunities to improve on their talents, and develop new skills. Parents need to be aware of weak areas in their lives, and help to strengthen them. This promise ensures that if they are properly trained, they will not stray from it.

HONOUR AND RESPECT

It is important to teach our children to honour and obey their parents. It is up to us as parents to make sure that they do this. God promises that things will go well for them if they do. (Ephesians 6:2) As parents take their responsibility to ensure this, the children become more aware of the boundaries and what is expected of them, this makes them more accountable. This will help children to be obedient when they are with you and also when you are not around.

Alongside that they need to learn to respect authority, whether it is school, police, Sunday school and youth leaders or the Pastor. We are living in a generation that has virtually no respect for authority, but if our children are to be mighty in God we need to train them about the things that are important to God. Teach them to respect older people, to be polite, and answer properly. And of course, parents lead by example.

PARENTS SERVE THE LORD

As parents you need to serve the Lord yourself, with gladness. It's a Biblical principle to be committed to a local church, and serve there. We all have something to bring and something to give. Many Christian parents are not committed and drift from church to church, sending their children to camps and youth clubs hoping this will "Do the Trick". I can tell you now it won't! You need to be fully serving God yourself and bringing your children with you. Take responsibility to teach your children how to behave in church, and to listen and respect the Sunday school teachers and Pastor.

Talk with them about the work that is being done around the world through missionaries and evangelism. Tell them about the men and women of the past who have done great things for God and help them have a desire to serve God. Teach them about faithfulness and commitment, and how God honours it. Teach them to honour the five-fold ministry and to draw from their gifts. According to Ephesians 4:11-12 they have been given to mature and equip the people of God. So you and your children need to receive everything they have to impart into your lives. Never speak against men and women who serve God. (1 Chronicles 16:22) Always seek to help and encourage them in the move of God, and teach your children to do the same. Be submissive, to go against them is to make yourself a burden to them and that is no advantage to you and your children. It actually puts you at a disadvantage. So train your children to be hungry for a move of God and to serve in it whole-heartedly.

ROLE MODELS

Teenagers look for role models. How do I know? Take a look at most of their bedroom walls and there you'll see posters of singers, TV personalities, sports people and film stars. They are a constant reminder to them of the people that they admire, and want to be like. They are looking for someone to look up to, someone to imitate. We need to encourage true role models for our children. People of integrity, serving God wholeheartedly, who they can look up to and say, "I would like to be like that when I am older". Parents you need to be wise about who is influencing your children and teenagers. Be careful to make sure that older people around your children are people who are going to bring a godly influence, because whether we like it or not they will bring some kind of influence. Be wise about what kind of influences you allow into your home, and be aware to whom your growing children are looking up.

SPIRITUAL PARENTS

Recently I saw a teenage boy staggering, trying to stand up. Obviously he had too much to drink. I looked around to see his father. He was in a worse state, unable to raise another glass to his lips. The Holy Spirit immediately spoke to my heart, "he has no role model". I saw a young man, in the prime of his life, with no one to be an example for him to follow, no spiritual father. Our world is full of young people like that teenage boy. Parents, God may require you to reach out and be a spiritual mother or father, giving wise counsel and support, and being to a young person what a godly parent should be. Without that in their lives, they are left wide open to all the enticement of the world, only to be left hurt and disappointed that it doesn't bring the fulfillment for which they had hoped. Are you willing to take your place and stand in that gap for somebody else's child? I believe as we rise up and trust the power of the Holy Ghost to anoint us to do this task, there are thousands upon thousands of lives that can be transformed for the glory of God.

TEACH YOUR CHILDREN TO BE KIND

We need to train our children to be kind and have a heart of compassion for others. This is something that is caught rather than taught. As they see you reaching out to others they will want to follow your example. Jesus Himself was filled with compassion, (Mark 1:41) and that lead to action. He was ready to minister and pray for people everywhere He went. As you reach out and have a heart for others, your children will follow in your footsteps. Include them when you pray for others. Let them pray with you. Encourage them to lay their hands on people with you, and let them see the power of God heal and set people free.

LEAD BY EXAMPLE

When I was a child I walked about a mile to school each day. Once a week I was given a container full of food. Every Thursday on my way to school I took the meal to an old man called Mr. Smith. He seemed extremely old to me, and bent over. His wife had recently died, and he was alone. As long as Mr. Smith lived on his own he had a meal from our house every week. As well as that, we never sat down to our Christmas meal without first taking him his. It would be piping hot, on a tray, and raced by car just ready for the frail old man to enjoy.

Then there were Friday afternoons. That was the time my mother visited the sick and elderly in our village. On Saturday evenings my father would join her, and as he could drive they would be able to travel further to visit the sick.

As I grew older they would take me with them. I had just started learning to play the guitar, and could manage three chords and two songs, "Amazing Grace" and "What a friend we have in Jesus". As I accompanied my parents on these visits, I would play, and sing softly to these people, and then pray with them. We knew nothing back then about healing and baptism of the Holy Spirit and faith like we know today. But we did know that Jesus loves us and died to save us. We took the little we had and God used it to bless others, some in the last weeks and months of their lives.

My point is this. My mother led by example. Without realizing it she helped me have a love for people, and taught me to be kind and caring. We need to teach our children to care for others. Lead by example, and give them opportunity alongside you. As they see compassion in your heart, it will touch their lives. Teach them that serving God is a wonderful adventure. God wants to use them. They are important now, not just when they are adults. Perhaps there is someone elderly, or in need that you can bless, and let your children be a blessing to them also. When our children were small we would go to the nursing homes nearby. We would sing carols and the children would sing and minister the love of God with those old people. It was wonderful to see them holding their hands and sharing the love of God with them. Give your children opportunities to be a blessing and watch God use them.

The dictionary informs us that character is a distinctive feature or quality, a moral strength. Developing Godly character is a process for all of us, including our children. It includes progressing in maturity, becoming more stable and secure, and having great integrity. These qualities will bring a moral strength. In the next chapter we will continue to look at character training, particularly in the area of attitudes. And remember, character produces winners.

CHAPTER THREE

ATTITUDE, ATTITUDE, ATTITUDE

Our attitude is our way of thinking, which is demonstrated by our behaviour. Proverbs 23:7 tells us, "For as he thinks in his heart, so is he". Whatever we are thinking will eventually come out, whether in our speech or behaviour. A person who thinks, "I'm a failure, I'll never amount to anything" will not attempt much, he has already decided what he is. Whereas a person who thinks, I can do all things through Christ who strengthens me. God is for me, who can be against me?" will attempt new assignments with great confidence.

In this chapter we are going to look at the importance of our attitude, and how to help our children develop a right attitude to themselves and their abilities, to God and to other people, and to tasks and challenges they will be faced with in life.

CHARACTER V GIFTS

As parents we should always encourage character above gifts. It is wonderful to have gifts. They are given by God and should be encouraged and developed. But as someone has already said, "Our gift will take us where our character won't keep us." It is far more important for our children to be reliable and responsible, handling things wisely for their age, than to be the best at a specific talent. Let's look at two examples:

1) A boy is a tremendous football player, everyone wants him on their team. But he has a vicious temper. Anytime the slightest thing goes wrong, or he looses the ball he flares up, curses at the referee, or attacks other players. Of course he is sent off. He cannot cope with losing or not getting his own way.

2) A young lady has a brilliant musical ability. She plays instruments and sings. Her gifts would be an asset to any music team. But she will not submit to any form of authority. Demanding her own way, and being only being interested in her own agenda, she causes problems for the choirmaster, and will not co-operate with the music team.

In both these cases the character has not been matured and developed. The selfish way these two people think made their needs more important than the good of the whole group. This has left them with a wonderful gift, but no one to whom they can share it, because they cannot work in a selfless way with others. They are insecure and demanding their own way, refusing to submit to authority, and their attitudes have let them down.

GUARD YOUR HEART

"Keep and guard your heart with all vigilance and above all that you guard, for out of it flow the springs of life." Proverbs 4:23 Amp.

We need to help guard our children's minds. They are like sponges. They will soak up what is put in front of them. Parents need to be careful what they watch on T.V. If we allow them to see too much violence, strife and sex, we are not guarding their hearts, and it will affect their attitude.

1 Corinthians 14:10 tells us that there are many kinds of voices in the world and all of them have an effect. If our children are listening to worldly music it will have an effect on their heart. No one can love God with all their heart and be filling their minds with the world's way of thinking. We need to help our children by making sure they have plenty of Christian music that they enjoy. Music plays a big part in most teenager's lives, so let's make sure that the music they listen to is filled with life and not death. Remember, "Death and life are in the power of the tongue and those who love it will eat its fruit". The words that our children listen to over and over again through music will have an effect on them. We need to take our responsibility to ensure that they listen to words of life and blessing.

A THANKFUL HEART

Today in the western world our children have more gadgets, increasing opportunities, more leisure and travel, and more designer clothes, yet we have become a complaining, grumbling society.

Mothers will push trolleys through huge supermarket isles, choosing anything off the shelves they want, and moan that they have to shop again, while our brothers and sisters in third world countries are struggling to survive, going from one major disaster to another, dying by the thousands.

We need to keep a thankful heart ourselves and encourage our children to do the same. Ask them regularly what has blessed them, and what they can thank God for. Teach them to appreciate the blessings that they have in their lives. When they are overflowing with thankfulness they can't be moaning and groaning.

Recently I was out walking and I heard beautiful singing coming from a small bird. I looked up through the branches of a tree. The bird sang so sweetly it attracted my attention. But when I spotted it, it was just an ordinary brown sparrow, making such a sweet sound. It spurred me on, and I thought if a scruffy little sparrow can sing it's heart out to God, then so can I. Encourage all your household to be praisers, with the gratitude attitude. And don't forget to be one yourself.

THE IMPORTANCE OF GOOD FRIENDS

"Bad company corrupts good character." 1 Cor. 15:33

It doesn't matter how responsible and strong your child's character is. If they are running around with bad company their character will be corrupted. Train your children to look for good friends. If there aren't any pray and ask God to provide them. Trust Him and believe for wise friends.

"He who walks with the wise men is wise, but a companion of fools will be destroyed." Proverbs 13:20

Here we are told that a companion of fools will be destroyed. A fool in the Bible is someone who is disobedient and unbelieving. If your child spends a lot of time with foolish peers, it will bring destruction. Don't be afraid to say "No" to friends who are going to bring a harmful influence to your child. You have wisdom that your children don't have, and can see pitfalls ahead of time. It is better to say "No" and save them from harm than to have a damaging situation to deal with later.

Parents really need wisdom in this area. Not all children who come to church are going to be good company for your child. Be wise and God will supply good friends that will be a blessing to your child and your home.

"I am a companion of all those who fear You. And of those who keep your precepts." Psalm 119:63

Don't feel you have to have everyone in your home. It is to be a place of peace, security and blessing. If other children come into my home and are bad mannered, with no respect I don't have them back. You are not to be walked on just because you are Christians. So guard your home and encourage good company for your children.

MONEY MAKES THE WORLD GO ROUND

Money may not make the world go round, but it is seriously important in our lives. Teach your children the Biblical principles about tithing and offering. Children will happily tithe their pocket money, when they know that the first ten percent belongs to God.

Train them to be wise with money, to save and not just spend all at once. Let them save for something special that they would really like. That helps them to appreciate things much more. Remember you are training them for the future and not just for now. Consistent principles that you lay down now, will be applied automatically as they get older.

SERVANT OF ALL

Children should be taught to help and serve around the home. Teach them to do a job thoroughly. Meal times are a good opportunity for them to help. They should soon volunteer without being asked. In our home everyone helped with housework, attending the garden and cleaning the car. We all used and enjoyed the benefits of them, therefore we all helped to maintain them. Pocket money was given separately for their own spending and saving. It was not associated with helping. These were responsibilities we all had and would undertake without payment. Always encourage your child when they help and especially when they do so without being asked.

> **"The faithful shall abound with blessings."**
> **Proverbs 28:20**

Teach them to be diligent and to finish a task properly. This principle will bring them great reward in life. But on the other hand being lazy will also have a consequence. So make sure you guard them from apathy and laziness. Faithfulness means being reliable and dependable. It implies that a person is thorough and can be completely counted on to tackle a task efficiently. This kind of adult is extremely valuable to a company, business or ministry. But it all begins with being trained at home to be faithful.

> **"Lazy hands make a man poor, but diligent hands bring wealth." Proverbs 10:4**

KEEP DECEIT OUT

Truthfulness and honesty are going to be vital for our children if they are going to walk closely with the Lord. We need to walk in integrity ourselves and teach it to our children.

I remember as a child of about seven years old coming home from school to my father and telling him rather excitedly that I had copied someone else's work and got everything right. I thought I had discovered a wonderful way to always achieve top results. My father was very wise. He sat down and explained to me that this way of achieving had a name. It was called "cheating" and that I should never do it. If I could not do my work I was to ask my teacher for help, but I was never to copy because that made me a cheat. I never forgot his words of wise counsel and as far as I remember I never cheated again in schoolwork.

He taught me another valuable lesson about honesty when I was a teenager. I told him I was going to a local football match. But instead of going in through the main entrance and having to pay, I would hop over the fence, at the back of our house and slip in unnoticed through the hedge. No one would know, and I would get in free. Again he took the time to tell me that this was completely dishonest. If I wanted to go to the match I must pay like everyone else. Under no circumstances could I be dishonest. These principles have really stood to me in life. God requires that we walk uprightly before Him, with nothing hidden in our lives. We need to train our children to speak truthfully and be honest before God and men, then they will have nothing to hide and no reason to be ashamed.

ENCOURAGE GOOD CHARACTER

Be a great encouragement to your child when you see them taking initiative to help without being asked, forgiving when they are feeling hurt, choosing God's way in a situation, instead of their own, and not bowing to peer pressure. These are all signs of a maturing, secure character, and as parents, we need to make sure we encourage them. When they make wise choices for their age and are diligent in schoolwork, or show kindness to an elderly relative, these are all signs of maturing character that we need to encourage. Children thrive on encouragement. In fact adults do as well. Lets make sure we give our children plenty of it. They should never have to wonder whether we are pleased with them, we should always make sure that we let them know. Never compare your child with another. They are unique and different. What one child finds easy may be of extreme difficulty for another. When a child works hard at something and has done their best they should be applauded, even if it is not of the same standard as another child. The importance is in seeing that the child has done the best that they could at that stage of their lives. Criticism can lead to discouragement and a feeling of not wanting to try for fear of not being able to match up to someone else. So always ensure that your child never suffers from a lack of encouragement.

PERSEVERANCE

Help your child to develop a persevering attitude. Train them not to give up too quickly. Anyone who has done anything great in life has had to persevere and get back up again after failing. We are not helping our children if we opt for the easy way out or the quick solution. Sport is a great opportunity for them to persevere, as well as good exercise, and using some of their young energy. It also helps them work with others, as a team, and to take turns. They learn to handle losing and disappointments, and being gracious in victory. They have opportunities to push themselves physically and will look back with great satisfaction at the skills they have learned and the fun they had.

HAND OF THE DILIGENT

"He who has a slack hand becomes poor, But the hand of the diligent makes rich." Proverbs 10:4

Training our children to work hard and be diligent will bring blessing into their lives. They need to learn to be good stewards and look after their room, toys, bike, pet, etc. Our children also need to be responsible in their schoolwork, working to the best of their ability, and being consistent.

The Bible also teaches that the faithful shall abound with blessings, and that he who is faithful in little shall be ruler over much. If our children want responsibility for more they must first show that they are reliable and trustworthy with little. It is a biblical principle for us all.

SOUR GRAPES

Jeremiah 31:29 tells us that the fathers have eaten sour grapes and it has set the children's teeth on edge. As parents if we are bitter about something and hold unforgiveness it sours our lives and affects our children. It is like a poison that will automatically spread to our children and contaminate them. We need to walk in forgiveness continually and keep our hearts right towards others. Always speak well of others. Make a decision not to gossip or speak negatively, but to always believe the best of everyone. Don't allow others to come into your home and slander, mock or belittle anointed men of God. Make sure you keep the sour grapes away.

If we desire to be all that God has intended for us to be then our attitudes will need to line up with His Word. Much of our children's attitudes will be "caught" from us. They can be the cause of victory or failure, of Godliness or compromise, and even life or death. What better place for them to develop attitudes that please God than in the home, where their hearts and minds can be guarded. They can grow up unpolluted by the world, and having the mind of Christ, so that they can fully respond to all that God has for their lives.

Through all our lives there is the opportunity to get hurt, disappointed and offended. It's the same for our children. We need to help them to walk in love and forgive. Make sure no root of hurt develops in their hearts and prevent it from growing into bitterness and hatred. Teach them to let go of hurt, and forgive. God is much bigger than what has happened to them. As they focus their attention on the faithfulness of God, He will be their defender. Psalm 37:6 tells us that he will bring forth your righteousness as the light, and the justice of your cause like the noon-day sun. So use it as an opportunity to help them grow in forgiveness, and to trust in God. Then they are in a position to move on with their life, instead of being soured with bitterness. Unforgiveness and bitterness can effect so many relationships, it really does sour our lives, and is often brought into marriages and future relationships. Barriers are put up like huge fences around people's lives to protect themselves from ever getting hurt again. Many decide never to allow anyone to get close for the fear of being hurt and let down. So it is vital that we teach our children how to handle situations like this, in order for them not to have problems in their future relationships.

CHAPTER FOUR

DISCIPLINE AND DELIVER

None of us can live a successful life without discipline. We need it when we turn off the alarm each morning, in order to arrive at work on time. Students need to be disciplined to study for their exams. We may need to discipline our eating habits if we want to keep those extra pounds off. And we need to discipline our lives if we want to learn new skills for that promotion at work. All of us need discipline. Without it we cannot accomplish much. It can make us or break us.

DON'T SET YOUR HEART ON DESTRUCTION

"Chasten your son while there is still hope. And do not set your heart on his destruction." Proverbs 19:18

As parents we would never want to deliberately turn our children towards their own destruction, but that is what the Bible says we are doing if we withhold discipline from them. When I withhold discipline from my child, I am actually setting my heart on their destruction. So as parents we need to take the responsibility of disciplining our children very seriously. The book of Proverbs is full of wisdom in so many areas. There we will find the way to discipline our children, and therefore bring great blessing to our household.

"Foolishness is bound up in the heart of a child. The rod of correction will drive it far from them." Proverbs 22:15

I remember discovering this verse many years ago and feeling I had found an amazing treasure. "Foolishness is bound up in the heart of a child", so that's what it is, now I understood. I had these two lovely toddlers, at this stage, beautiful children, naturally inquisitive, but something was wrong. Then I discovered that foolishness was in their heart, which, by this time was obvious to me. My job was to drive it far from them. This became apparent to me one day when I had left them standing on a chair at the kitchen sink allowing them to play with their tea set. I was busy attending to something else. Perhaps it was the new baby that had recently arrived. When I returned I found them squealing at the top of their voices, "Weee!!!! swimming pool". They were taking it turns to fill a cup with water and pour it all over the kitchen floor. And yes by this time it did look like a swimming pool. And, in case you are wondering I did get out the rod of discipline and spank them with it. You may think that was rather harsh. But they knew it was wrong. Both they and I knew if I had been standing in the kitchen they would have never done that. It was only when my back was turned that they thought they could get away with it. We laugh about it now, but I know that the discipline that I gave them then had a tremendous effect on the people they are today. And it never happened again. What a relief. I could actually do something about it. Not only that but God held me responsible to do something about it. I could actually remove the foolishness from their heart by discipline. I believe if you discipline properly the incident will not occur again. Many times parents make the mistake of not disciplining and the same incidents occur over and over again. Something is seriously wrong here. If you find yourself in that position you need to check how you are disciplining your children. Parents should never persuade or plead with their children to get them to obey. Children should be taught from a very young age that disobedience is punished. It is not something that is argued about. The parents communicate what is expected, the children keep within those boundaries otherwise there is discipline.

THE CONSEQUENCES OF FOOLISHNESS

The book of Proverbs also teaches us about fools. They will despise your words of wisdom. Proverbs 23:9 It does not matter how much wisdom you put in front of them, they don't want it and will not receive it. They are deliberately disobedient, and keep returning to their own folly, repeating their mistakes, just like a dog returns to its vomit (Proverbs 26:11). A fool will end up despising his parents and having no discernment – (Proverbs 15:20-21). That is not the end result any of us want to see for our children. So we need to look at discipline seriously, as God has planned it for us, so that our children can live in the blessing and benefit of it, and foolishness be driven far from them. A lack of discipline means that we can be well on the way to raising fools, and none of us wants to be responsible for that.

SHAME AND EMBARRASSMENT

"The rod and rebuke give wisdom. But the child left to himself brings shame to his mother." Proverbs 29:15

We can see from this verse that if we do not take our responsibility to rebuke and discipline our children the consequence is to bring shame and embarrassment on the parents.

We need to help our children to see that discipline and correction is actually going to bless them and keep them within safe boundaries, for themselves and the welfare of other people. Proverbs 12:1 (Amp) is clarity itself, "Whoever loves instruction and correction loves knowledge, but he who hates reproof is like a brute beast, stupid and indiscriminating". We need to take time to explain the benefits of discipline, and the blessing of obedience to our children, and of course, alongside that we should be building a close relationship of love and affection.

ELI AND HIS SONS

We read an example of the consequences of not disciplining children in the life of Eli, found in 1 Samuel 3:12. We see here that Eli did not restrain his sons, even though he knew he should. As we read on we see that God judged his household because of the sin in which his sons continued. His two sons died suddenly and the Ark of the Covenant was taken. When Eli heard that they had died, he too died. All because he did not take his responsibility to deal with the sin in his own home, and discipline his sons. In the end it became his downfall and the downfall of his two sons.

DISCIPLINE AND DELIVER

A child who is being teachable will not need discipline to correct him, but he may need an explanation. For example: "No you cannot play with the video because you might break it". "These are your toys, you may play with these".

A child who is being willfully disobedient closes off effective teaching and needs firm loving discipline, otherwise this behaviour will disrupt the harmony of the family.

"Do not withhold correction from a child, for if you beat him

with a rod he will not die. You shall beat him with a rod, and deliver his soul from death." Proverbs 23:13-14

The Bible makes it clear that while discipline may be painful it should never be injurious. Never is harm to be inflicted on children, but pain will undoubtedly be felt as part of corrective discipline. A child's eternal destiny can hinge upon whether parents will take their responsibility and discipline. Discipline, when necessary, should be administered to the backside! The best place for it! Parents should never lash out and hit a child unexpectedly. The child should know the boundaries. It is the parent's responsibility to explain them. Discipline should be used for willful disobedience, rebellion and stubbornness.

MEAN WHAT YOU SAY - SAY WHAT YOU MEAN

Make sure you mean what you say. A child will then know, if I disobey I will be punished, and it will be painful. Both parents and child should know the boundaries. It is up to the parents to set them and communicate them to the child. Many times the parents give an instruction but don't really mean it. We say to our child, "Do not climb that tree". Two minutes later, when our back is turned, and we are deep in conversation with someone, the child is happily swinging from the tree. The parent ignores it. They have just taught their child that he can disobey and get away with it. His mother doesn't really mean what she says. He can do his own thing and get away with it.

Another example is a mother telling the little girl to tidy away her toys. Mother leaves the room and carries on with the dishes. Ten minutes later mother is in the back in the sitting room expecting to see the toys almost cleared away. "Oh, I thought I told you to tidy up your toys. It's time for your bath now, so pack up your things," she urges, a little more firmly. Five minutes later the child is still playing, and the mother yells at the top of her voice, "Put those toys away NOW!" The child learns that the mother doesn't really mean what she says the first time, and the child can get away with disobedience. The child only has to obey when the mother loses her temper. Parents need to mean what they say the first time, and expect obedience.

> **"He who spares the rod hates his son. But he who loves him disciplines him promptly." Proverbs 13:24**

Disciplining our children promptly according to this scripture is actually, loving them. Rather then waiting until the "last straw", when we feel exasperated and ready to "blow a fuse".

GOD MEANS WHAT HE SAYS

It is so important that our children know that we mean what we say. God means what he says, and he expects to be obeyed. There is no blessing for us without obeying Him. Your children will have difficulty in obeying God if they do not learn to obey you first. Look at your children when you speak to them. Get them to look back at you so that they fully listen and understand you.

Set your children small tasks, which they can accomplish, and ask them to come and tell you when they are finished. This teaches them to be accountable and to finish a job properly. Teach them to tidy up after their activities. Even a toddler can learn to put a few toys away. You can lead by example and then get them to do it for you. Always praise and encourage them when they listen and obey. Listening and obeying is what God requires of us, according to Deuteronomy 28:1, in order for the blessings of God to overtake us. So in training them in this way, you are not only taking great order and harmony in your home, but you are shaping their lives for the future.

TEMPER TANTRUMS

Never allow temper tantrums, and never reward them with sweets or toys in order to stop the outbreak quickly. This may seem an easy way out, and calm the child down rapidly, but it has also taught the child they can be obnoxious and get their own way. If a parent consistently allows that, the child will get used to demanding their own way through mood swings, tantrums and manipulation. This kind of behaviour causes a child to have social problems later on, when they find it extremely difficult to cope with not getting their own way. It can result in depression and extreme mood swings. Don't give in to children's whining and moaning. Teach them to accept "no" without grumbling. "No, we are not buying chocolate today, we had some yesterday". Stick to it! Don't allow yourselves to be manipulated by everything they want.

A child will thrive on structure, order and discipline. They know their boundaries and if trained properly will want the rewards of living with them. How you discipline at home and the behaviour you tolerate will emerge eventually in public, probably in the middle of a supermarket or when you are visiting a friend's house. So train your child at home first, if you want them to behave when they are out. For example if you allow them to be cheeky and answer you back at home then they will be sure to repeat elsewhere. If you allow mood swings and temper tantrums, someone else has to deal with it when they start school or in a friend's home. So whatever we allow at home will eventually emerge outside it.

THE REWARDS OF DISCIPLINE

"No discipline seems pleasant at the time, but is painful. Later on, however, it will produce a harvest of righteousness and peace for those who have been trained by it."(Hebrews 12:11)

There is a wonderful harvest for both you and your children when you apply discipline the way God has directed it.

This virtue will produce peace and righteousness, and you will be so glad you undertook your responsibility. Biblical discipline challenges our modern philosophies and practices of child rearing. But as you train up your children to obey you, honour authority and follow instructions they will bring great blessing to your life. You will have rest and peace about your children instead of anxiety and dread. They will be as Proverbs 29:17 says "A delight to your soul".

CHAPTER FIVE

LOVE AND ENCOURAGEMENT

Alongside discipline and training, there must also be a balance of love, affection and encouragement. Tell your child that you love him, and that he is special to you, and to God. Show affection and make time for you to be close. If you were brought up with no affection shown to you, don't let that carry on to your children. Bring them close and hug them often, they really need it.

Hebrews 3:13 tells us to encourage one another daily. Encouragement will help them persevere in things, and bring a strength to their lives. Showing genuine interest in our children's achievement, whether it's sport, music, school work etc it is so important. When we visit their schools, go to the parents evening, watch them in a match or on stage, we are getting involved in their world. That speaks so loudly to our children. It tells them "your world matters to me, I care about you." It's important for fathers as well as mothers to get involved. That may mean sometimes taking time off work, or putting other things aside, but it demonstrates to our children that they are a priority to us. We need to make sure we're not too busy for them. How many parents look back and say "I wish I'd spent more time with them." Very few, if any say, "I wish I'd spent more time at the office!"

A parent noticed their child was struggling badly in school. The father became angry with his son, frustrated at the child's low marks. Term by term the marks went down. The father realized his attitude with the boy was making things worse. So he spent some time with him, looking at each subject. Math 30% "It's better than 20%" the

Father would say. "But if you work a little harder at it and I help you maybe next term we could get up to 35% or even 40%." The child and his father went through every subject with the father encouraging him, if he worked harder he could do it. What a wise man. He was saying, "Son I believe in you. I believe you can put more effort in, I'm with you all the way." Slowly, but surely that child's results improved. By the time he left school he had done extremely well and went on to third level education. Encouragement works!

1 Corinthians 13:1-8 describes love. It's good to take inventory sometimes of how our love walk is going in the home. There all our barriers are down and we don't always appreciate the people God has put around us. Children are a gift from God. His love is patient and kind, we're going to need lots of those qualities when raising a family. But Romans 5:5 tells us that His love has already been shed abroad in out hearts. We already have it. We just have to walk in it. Love never fails, so it will not fail us as we put it into practice.

HAVE YOU GOT THE TIME?

Spending quality time with our children is so important, and it starts when they are young. Reading to them and looking at books together develops a closeness. Taking a few moments each day out of our busy schedule to play their choice of games involves us in their world.

As our children grow older it is equally important for us to be there for them, to listen, encourage and talk with them. We need to know where they are, not just whose home they are in or what match they are watching. We have a responsibility as parents to know where they are emotionally, and spiritually.

The Holy Spirit will help you to be discerning about your child as you depend on Him. We need to be aware of the struggles they are going through, the disappointments, as well as the dreams in their heart.

Finishing each day on a happy note helps to build security and stability into their lives. It's a time to pray, read the Bible, thank God for His goodness, and assure our children of God's love and our love for them.

THE WONDERFUL TEENAGE YEARS

Your children's teenage years can be a wonderful time of growing closer as friends while they are growing more independent of you.

We found it helpful to take each child individually away for a few days before they started secondary school. I would take the girls, and Sean took our son. This was a time where we could give our undivided attention to them. During those times we would discuss many of the issues they would be facing in their teenage years. It was a time of preparation for them. We would discuss different areas such as peer pressure, and how to handle it. Sexuality and God's ways compared to the world's ways. We would look at the effects of mood swings that teenagers can sometimes face and the fact that many teenagers face depression, and have a tendency to swing from one extreme to the other, depending on who they are with and how things are in their lives. It is a time of uncertainty and change, as parents it is very important that we help them to cope with it effectively. Friendship was another topic we covered, and the importance of finding and being a good friend. And of course, we looked at what happens when friends let you down. Generally we were taking time out of our schedule to look at the situations that were surrounding their lives and helping them to cope with it. Being forewarned is a great help when someone is going through a difficulty. Sometimes later on when a situation arose we would be able to say, "Do you remember when we discussed this, and talked about what we would do if this situation arose." It was a great help to have already discussed it and to have looked at ways of handling it. It was also a time for developing togetherness. A key through child rearing years is to keep your family close. This is one way of achieving this.

Teenage years can be wonderful if we take the time to prepare for them, and keep our family close in their relationships before they enter teenage years and during them.

SECURE HOMES

> **"My people will live in peaceful dwelling places, in secure homes, in undisturbed places of rest." Isaiah 32:18 N.I.V.**

God's wants our families to live in peaceful, secure homes, without strife and confusion. There our children can develop in character, as well as physically and emotionally and reach their full potential.

It is VITALLY important for mothers to keep a calm and gentle spirit, as they are the ones that usually set the mood of the home. 1 Peter 3:4 Tells us that the unfading beauty of a calm and gentle spirit is precious in the sight of God. If God places so much importance on a calm and gentle spirit then so should we. It in no ways implies weakness. In Proverbs 31:10-31 we read that the virtuous wife is clothed with strength and honour, she works hard and knows what is going on in the life of her household. Her worth is absolutely priceless. These qualities will produce a stable, peaceful environment for those within her home.

PARENTS LOVE FOR GOD

"You shall love the Lord your God with all your heart, with all your soul and with all your strength. And these words which I command you today shall be in your heart. You shall teach them diligently to your children, and shall talk of them when you sit in your house, when you walk by the way, when you lie down, and when you rise up." Deuteronomy 6:5-7

The secret of raising our children for God is always centered around us having a sincere heart of love for Him, which always involves us being obedient. There is no way we can have the results that God desires if we do not do things His way. Deuteronomy 6:5 tells us we are to love Him with our heart, soul and strength, that seems to me like everything we've got! When we do that we will know first hand His commands and ways, and what He requires of us. Our hearts will be full of his words and we will want to communicate them to our children.

GOD'S GOT YOU COVERED

God, not only requires, but He demands us to be diligent in teaching His ways to our children. In other words, it will not just happen, we have to make sure it happens. We cannot do that unless we spend time with them. Sitting around the kitchen table or at their bedside at night are all opportunities to talk about the Lord. These should be natural because out of the heart the mouth speaks. (Matthew 12:34) If our hearts are fully on the ways of God, we should automatically share them with our children but in case we don't God has commanded us to be diligent about talking of His ways to our children. Traveling in the car, taking them to school, meal times, bed times are all opportunities to share the things of God with them.

We found that praying together each morning as a family is most important. As children grow each one can take a turn to lead that time, having a scripture to share and something to impart to the rest of the family. We encourage them all to speak in tongues every day. The Bible says it edifies and gives spiritual strength as well as speaking mysteries and secret revelations of God. (1 Corinthians 14:2) Our children need all the strength and help they can get before they go out into the world each day. This is one way of ensuring that they get it.

Last thing at night it is important to pray with them, and read the scriptures, perhaps just one verse that you can help them apply to their lives.

GOD BELIEVES IN YOU

God has really entrusted you with an incredible responsibility in raising and shaping young lives. He has entrusted you to be extremely careful to follow His specific directions. He believes in you. You can do it!

MEAL TIMES

Meal times can be made into special occasions. It is good to try to have at least one meal together a day as a family. This is fast becoming a thing of the past. But God requires unity, trust and fellowship in our lives. Eating together regularly helps to build that. Meal times can be made special in simple ways. During our damp, dark, Irish winters we always have lots of candles at our dinner table. People who have dropped in unexpectedly have asked if I have someone special coming for dinner. I have often been tempted to say, "Oh no, it's just the family!" But now that I realize how important to God our family is I have changed my reply to, "Oh yes, we have some very special people coming for dinner today!"

Meal times are occasions of sharing the events of the day. Maybe everyone can share something positive. "The best thing that happened today, or this week was...." Sometimes in giving thanks for food you can encourage everyone to have something for which to thank God. These are all ways to build happy memories in the lives of our children as we seek to make our homes secure, peaceful dwelling places for our family in which to thrive. It is important to make them relaxed happy times when each member of the family can be themselves, and come in away from the world, and find warmth and acceptance, and a place where they belong.

BUILDING HAPPY MEMORIES

I was deeply moved recently while watching a documentary about a young family whose mother was diagnosed with terminal cancer. She had been given one year to live. The parents decided that they would spend that year together, as a family, going to lots of interesting places and having fun together while their mother was still alive. At the end of that year the mother died, as expected, and sometime later, the family were interviewed about how they had spent the previous year. The young teenage daughter was asked what were the best moments she spent with her mother while she was alive. The girl explained that her mother would get hungry in the middle of the night, because her eating pattern had changed. She would creep downstairs and eat a bowl of cereal.

When the daughter learned about this she asked her mother to wake her so that they could go downstairs together to eat cereal. Her mother did this and they had many times of eating cereal at two o'clock in the morning. When asked what were the highlights of the last year with her mother, it wasn't the wonderful trips and expensive holidays, it was the simple things that meant the most. The times when her mother would wake her while everyone else was asleep, and they would eat and chat together, to her, were the most precious moments of that year.

Building happy memories into our children's lives is not difficult to achieve. It is sometimes the simple things in our family lives that bring us close, and mean the most to our children. We need to make sure we do not overlook them. They are more valuable than we may realize.

OUR HOLY SPIRIT HELPER

As parents we have a wonderful friend and counsellor, the Holy Spirit, standing by 24 hours a day. Learn to ask for His help and depend on him while you are training your children. He will give you wisdom and insight and enable you to reach the heart of your child. He will show you pitfalls ahead of time, so that you can steer your child around them. Being sensitive to the Holy Spirit will enable you to be close to your child, causing a special bond and trust to develop. As you walk with the Holy Spirit you will be anointed to be the best parent you can be for your child. (John 14:26)

CHAPTER SIX

GOOD-BYE MR AVERAGE

If you are going to be a parent who has supernatural results you can forget about being average, and fitting in with the crowd. Being easily intimidated will hold you back from your God given destination. It will stop you walking in the authority that God has planned and make you easily manipulated.

This is for the man or woman who greatly delights in God's way. He loves God so much He will do anything he can to put His ways into practice. For this man his children will be powerful and blessed. (Psalm 112:1)

But in order to be a parent like that you may have to say good-bye to some traditions, or change some thought patterns. The Bible calls this "renewing our minds." (Romans 12:2) This is done by spending time meditating on the Word of God until we renew our thinking to God's way. Then we can teach them to our children. Don't just "go with the flow," find out God's principles, stick to them at all costs. Be prepared to teach them to your children. Don't just let them pick up the world's way.

Your children need to grow in an atmosphere where the presence of God and the goodness of God are evident. They need to know that sin always has a consequence, however attractive it may be, and that following God is a wonderful adventure in life.

There may be times in bringing up your children when you just do not know what to do. James 1:5 promises us that if we lack wisdom we can ask of God who gives to all men liberally. He reminds us not to doubt, but to ask in faith. He will give you direction and guide you through these years. Expect Him to direct your path as you ask for help. (Proverbs 3:6)

We need to take hold of God's ways, giving them our attention. Proverbs 4:20-22 reminds us not let them out of our sight, and to have God's ways in the midst of our heart. It's something we have to take responsibility for, and be diligent about.

GOD'S WAYS ARE HIGHER THAN OUR WAYS

"For my thoughts are not your thoughts, neither are my ways your ways, declares the Lord. As the Heavens are higher than the earth, so are my ways higher than your ways and my thoughts higher than your thoughts." Isaiah 55: 8-9

God's thoughts may not be our thoughts, but He has made it possible for us to gain His thoughts by giving us His Word. He is disclosing His thoughts, and His ways to us. That is why it is so important for us to renew our minds to His Word, and become confident in what God says, letting His Word dwell richly in us. Then we will have the mind of Christ and think His thoughts. This applies not just to bringing up children, but to every area of life.

GOD'S SECRETS

Did you know that God wants to reveal His secrets to you? Yes, God reveals His secret counsel to His close friends. (Psalm 25:14) He will also reveal things to you as you walk close enough to listen. That is why it is so important for us to guard our hearts, keeping out ungodly thoughts, negative attitudes, and offence. Then our heart is open and pure, enabling us to hear and receive the wonderful things that God has for us. (Psalm 119:18) He will give you understanding concerning your children, enabling you to have insight and direction, and warn of hidden dangers ahead of time. How sad when parents miss these things, simply because their hearts are not open to receive what the Holy Spirit wants to show them.

NO CURSE CAN LAND WITHOUT A CAUSE

"Like a flitting sparrow, like a flying swallow, so a curse without a cause cannot alight." Proverbs 26:2

Just as a sparrow has to have somewhere to land, like a branch or a rooftop, and a swallow who cannot take off from the ground, but must have an overhead wire or the side of a house. So a curse has to have a place to land. In other words the devil cannot come in on your family and land with a curse if there is no place to land.

One of the purposes in writing this book is to see that we give him no place to "land" his curses in the lives of our children. Of course, this applies to every area of life, our health, our business, God's protection etc. You can fool proof your family from the curses of the enemy and walk in the blessings of God if you are willing and obedient to His Word. This is wonderful news. The devil cannot just come in on my children and cause unbelief, rebellion and destruction.

I am protected by the Blood of Jesus, and Psalm 91 declares that if I dwell in the secret place of the Most High I shall abide under the shadow of the Almighty. He will be my refuge and fortress. I shall be delivered from any snare the devil has set for me. No plague or sickness can come in on me. If trouble does come He will deliver me. (verse 15) I'll have long life. There will be no sudden death for me or my children. He will show me His salvation, His goodness, and I will experience and partake of it. These promises are for you, your children, and your children's children!

"He remembers His covenant forever. The Word which He has commanded for a thousand generations." Psalm 105:8

We have a covenant with God. He keeps His promises with us as we walk in fellowship and obedience with Him. His promises cannot be broken. Jesus has paid for us to be set free by His own blood. We have to hold unswervingly to His promises, because He is faithful to us. Hebrews 10:23

So rise up from being Mr. or Mrs. Average, and allowing "Whatever will be will be" to come on your children. Get God's thoughts concerning your children. Stand on what He has promised, and He will bring it to pass.

CHAPTER SEVEN

DON'T BE AFRAID TO SAY "NO"

When we look at God as our perfect Father we see that right from the beginning He was not afraid to say "no" to His children. He said "no" to Adam regarding the tree in the garden.

The Lord God commanded the man, saying, "Of every tree in the garden you may freely eat: but of the tree of the knowledge of good and evil you shall not eat, for in the day that you eat of it you shall surely die." Genesis 2:16-17

When they did eat of the tree they were out of the garden, they lost fellowship with God, sin entered and they died spiritually. God had set limitations, and said "No" and man faced the consequences when he disobeyed.

There are many other times in scripture when God says "no" always for the benefit and protection of others. We see it when Lucifer wanted to ascend above the Lord and God said "No" and threw him out of heaven. We also see it in the life of King Saul, when he repeatedly disobeyed God, and in the end died in battle with his own sword. In the New Testament both Judas and also Ananias and Sapphira suffered the consequences of going against the things that God had said, interestingly in each case their lives were cut short. That makes me want to make sure that neither myself or my children go against the "No's" of God.

THE IMPORTANCE OF MEANING WHAT YOU SAY

We as parents need to mean what we say, and say what we mean. If we say no to something we need to be clear about it, and mean it. Our children soon get to understand when we mean what we say. They also sense the nuances if we are easily manipulated and don't really mean it. They know whether they can "twist us round their little finger" by moaning and whining and throwing tantrums. Many times they will give the impression "Everyone else is doing it." We need to be confident in what we have decided and stick with it.

EXPERIENCE AND WISDOM

Parents sometimes forget that they have something that their children do not have, experience, wisdom and maturity. This gives us insight and understanding. The years of experience enable us to understand where the pitfalls and hidden dangers are. Children will not be aware of them and need parents to put the limits on their lives to guard and protect them.

ELI AND SONS

We have already looked at the life of Eli the Priest regarding disciplining his sons. Now we will look at what happened in his life when he not only refused to discipline his sons, allowing them to continue in their sin openly, but also what happened when he would not say "No" to them. We read of the disastrous consequences of this in 1 Samuel 3:12-24

"In that day I will perform against Eli all that I have spoken concerning his house, from beginning to end."

"For I told him that I will judge his house forever for the impurity which he knows, because his sons made themselves vile and he did not restrain them."

"And therefore I have sworn to the house of Eli that the iniquity of the house of Eli shall not be atoned for by sacrifice or offering forever."1 Samuel 3:12-24

Eli lost his sons and his ministry. The Ark of the Covenant was taken, and the move of God in the earth was affected. All this happened because Eli knew of the sin in his sons' lives, but he refrained from restraining them.

When parents don't take responsibility to restrain and discipline their children they are in disobedience to God, and without exception, disobedience always has serious consequences.

There are times when we need to say "No" to our children. And parents when you say "No" you need to mean it. Children need to understand from a very young age that we mean what we say. It is very likely that Eli had not said no to his sons when they were younger, and by the time they were grown men he had no influence whatsoever on them.

TEACHING CHILDREN AND GRANDCHILDREN

> "Now this is the commandment and these are the statutes and judgments which the Lord your God has commanded to teach you, that you may observe them in the land which you are crossing to possess."
>
> "That you may fear the Lord your God and keep all His commandments which I command you and your son and your grandson, all the days of your life, and that your days may be prolonged." Deuteronomy 6:1-2

God is a God of the generations. He expects us to pass on His ways to our children and grandchildren. In fact, He not only expects it, He commands it. It is our God-given responsibility to do so. We will have to give account for it. In Deut 6:7 we are told to be diligent about teaching our children, there is to be nothing half-hearted or compromising about it.

TEACH THEM TO SAY NO

We need to teach them to say "NO" loud and clear. "No" to any form of compromise, or ungodliness, and "Yes" to God's way. If it is going to pull them away from God's way and the good plans that He has for them, then it is "No". There may be times that you will have to say no to some friends who are having a negative influence. Don't be afraid to do that and believe for some better friends. We don't choose our children's friends, but we can be wise and steer them away from companions with a negative influence.

"Blessed is the man who walks not in the counsel of the ungodly. Nor stands in the path of sinners, nor sits in the seat of the scornful: but his delight is in the law of the Lord, and on His law He meditates day and night." Psalm 1:1-2

God requires us to walk with Godly people, and to train our children to do the same. Other negative influences we need to train them to reject are TV and video programs, especially if they include too much strife, sex or violence.

Proverbs 4:23 tells us to guard our heart with all diligence, for out of it flows the issues of life. So just as we guard our own hearts, we also need to guard our children's hearts, especially in their formative years. Proverbs chapter 4 continues by saying in verse 24.

"Put away from you a deceitful mouth, and put perverse lips far from you. Let your eyes look straight ahead, and your eyelids look right before you." Proverbs 4:24

The Word of God says that we must say "No" to deceit, or gossip, or any kind of negative speaking that does not line up with what God says. Proverbs warns us that a mocker is a foolish person. We need to keep them from adopting mocking and sarcastic attitudes.

FRIENDS

As they get older your relationship changes to being more of a friend, and someone to whom they can confide. Be there to listen and encourage, and do things with your teenagers that they would enjoy. Perhaps browsing around the shops looking at things they like, or play a game of tennis, or sit up late at night talking. They need you to be with them more than ever. Try not to confront issues last thing at night, or as soon as they come home. Always send them off with a positive word, and always give them a warm welcome when they come in. Let them sleep peacefully, knowing that the words you have spoken have been kind and uplifting. When you build a loving, secure atmosphere, they won't want to go anywhere else for long.

DON'T LET SOMEONE ELSE PROGRAM THEIR MIND

In Psalm 101:3-4 the Psalmist decides that he will not look or partake of anything that is not right before God. He will have no perversity or wickedness anywhere near him, lest it should cling to him. That's a good stance to take with our children.

"I will set nothing wicked before my eyes: I hate the works of those who fall away: It shall not cling to me. A perverse heart shall depart from me: I will not know wickedness." Psalm 101:3

It is our responsibility to know what is influencing our children and to guard them from it. We need to make sure that we are not negligent in letting someone else program their fragile, developing minds.

Our children are not the way they are because of them. They are the way they are because of us. Let's make sure that we guard their hearts and minds. Let's say "No" to perverted thinking, which will put them on the course to destruction, and "Yes" to the values that will lead them to life.

CHAPTER EIGHT

JOYFUL SOUNDS

Be joyful. Make a decision about it! Make your home a joyful place to be. Laugh and sing around the home. Be fun to be with, your children should love coming home to you because of the cheerful atmosphere you create. Don't be over serious, even when things are serious.

> **"A merry heart does good like medicine. But a broken spirit dries the bones." Proverbs 7:22**

If you keep a merry (cheerful) heart it is going to do you and your household good. It's a tonic like good medicine. Most people today take vitamins and supplements in order to keep themselves well. It's particularly important when colds, chest problems and sore throats are prevalent. Parents will have the vitamins on the breakfast table ready for the family. Well how about taking a dose of cheerfulness along with the vitamins? Be cheerful, think cheerful, it will make a difference to your day and how you feel. Sometime ago I decided I needed to laugh. Life had been busy and sometimes we need to have a good laugh. So, I got out a funny video. It was one my children had seen, I had glanced at it but hadn't paid much attention to it. I was too busy with serious things to bother about such trivia! So, when I realized I needed to laugh I hired it, I got a bowl of popcorn and sat and laughed and laughed sometimes we need to have fun on purpose.

THE CONNECTION BETWEEN JOY AND STRENGTH

Did you know that there is a definite connection between joyfulness and strength? Check it up in your own life and you will see that when you're joyful you can accomplish so much, when your joy is low you feel down and you don't want to attempt to do much, it's all a great effort. The Bible tells us in Nehemiah 8:10

"The joy of the Lord is our strength."

We need all the strength we can get. God provides it by his joy. He wants us to be extremely joyful and that will overflow to our children. They need to be strong and fit for life. Joy is vitally important for them.

SOUNDS OF SINGING

"Oh sing to the Lord a new song. Sing to the Lord, all the earth. Sing to the Lord, bless his name. Proclaim the good news of his salvation from day to day. Declare his glory among the nations, his wonders among all people." Psalm 96:1-3

Here we are told to sing to the Lord. In fact he is speaking to all the earth. That includes parents and children. We are to sing and bless his name. We are to speak of his goodness everyday. As we walk with him his goodness and mercy will follow us. We need to expect it. Talk about it to your children and sing about it to the Lord. By singing of His goodness at home, your children will hear you and they will sing too. It gets into their heart and goes round their mind all day. It's wonderful to see them going off to school with a song of joy in their hearts. They will have it with them all day. There is such power in rejoicing in the Lord, so don't just wait until Sunday morning to praise and worship. Don't just listen to some one else praising on a CD. You do it. Magnify God and sing at the top of your voice and it will have a mighty effect on your children.

When our children were younger we had a time to pray together before they went out to school. Sometimes we would sing a song of thankfulness before they left home. We might even continue it on the way to school. I noticed on the mornings that we did that they would come home quietly humming or singing the same tune they had gone out with. So I tried an experiment. I would sing around the house about the goodness and faithfulness of God in the mornings, and in the evening it would still be on their minds, and somebody would be singing it unconsciously. Psalm 92 tells us to declare His loving kindness in the morning and His faithfulness at night. By singing out His goodness and love towards us our faith and expectancy grows. We expect His help, mercy and goodness to flow into our lives that day, and we are not disappointed.

REJOICING IN PRISON

"Rejoice in the Lord always, I will say it again - rejoice."
Phil 4:4

Paul wrote these words in a prison cell. He told the Philippians to rejoice and when they had done that, they were to rejoice again. In fact, he said we are to rejoice always. That means everyday, when we feel like it and when we don't. When things are going well, and when they aren't. When we are in prison like he was, and when we are free.

REJOICE, PRISON DOORS WILL OPEN

Paul knew the power of singing praises to God because when he and Silas were in prison they sang (Acts 16:16-40). Even though they had been severely beaten. It would be bad enough to be beaten at the hands of a soldier, but to be severely beaten was worse. They weren't let go either, but thrown into a cell, feet in stocks. There was no one rubbing antiseptic cream into the gashes on their backs. There was no ice to put on the bruises to take down the swelling. No nurse administered painkillers and no doctor was there ready to suture their wounds. But sitting in the prison, their bodies racked in pain, and aching, they began to sing and to pray and to pray and to sing. In fact they sang so loudly other prisoners heard it. God worked a mighty miracle, the doors were opened and their chains fell off. They were free to go.

JUST LIKE PAUL

God is no respecter of people. When you and I sing and praise, God can open the door for miracles - chains, bondages and things that hold us back lose their power. Sing with your children. Encourage them to worship with open hearts and hands raised in surrender to the Lord. As you draw near to God, He will draw near to you. You will see miracles done on your behalf, just as Paul did.

A THANKFUL HEART

I heard a story many years ago, which helped me so much in my own life, and in raising a family. I have told it many times. Each time I hear it I am inspired by it.

A young boy did not want to go to school because he had no shoes. He was afraid that the other children would laugh at him, being the only barefooted child in the school. His parents were sympathetic, but they could not afford shoes. They insisted that he must still go to school. His mother was concerned, and wondered how he was coping with the other children teasing him. All day she thought about him. When school ended she was there to meet him.
"How was school?" She anxiously asked.
"Did the children tease you?
Was it as difficult as you thought it would be?"
"Oh no," replied the boy, smiling,
"When I got to school with no shoes, I sat next to a boy with no feet. And I thought never mind about the shoes,
I'm just going to thank God for my feet."

THANKFULNESS LEADS TO JOY

The story speaks for itself. If we as parents are thankful, and encourage our children to be appreciative it can change everything. Thankfulness brings us from discouragement to joy. Joy, as we have already mentioned brings strength to our lives. Being thankful helps us enjoy the many blessings that come into our lives every day. The Bible says that God daily loads us with benefits. Let us appreciate and enjoy these blessings, and not allow them to pass us by unnoticed.

CHAPTER NINE

THE POWER OF YOUR CONFESSION

Right from the beginning of time words have played a powerful part in creation. We see that in creating the world God spoke and it happened.

According to Genesis chapter 1 after He had created the heavens and the earth the Holy Spirit was there, hovering over the face of the waters. The minute that God said, "Let there be light" the Holy Spirit and the Word worked together and there were millions of miles of light. God created everything by speaking, and the Holy Spirit was there to work with Him.

"By faith we understand that the worlds were framed by the Word of God, so that the things which are seen were not made of things which are visible." Hebrew 11:3

God arranged and set in order, and created the whole universe by His words. We are made in His image. Therefore our words have tremendous power when spoken in faith. We need to frame our children's world with the word of God.

IN YOUR HEART AND IN YOUR MOUTH

The first place we need to put God's Word is in our hearts and we do that by meditating over scripture, until we really get a revelation, and then it becomes a conviction. Colossians 3:10 tells us to let the word of God dwell in us richly, and we do this by giving it our attention.

GIVE HIS WORD ATTENTION

"My son give attention to my words: incline your ear to my sayings. Do not let them depart from your eyes: Keep them in the midst of your heart: For they are life to those who find them, and health to all their flesh".
"Keep your heart with all diligence,
for out of it springs the issues of life".
"Put away from you a deceitful mouth. And put perverse lips far from you." Proverbs 4: 20-24

Once we have given attention to what God says, faith will begin to operate in our hearts, because faith comes by hearing and hearing by the word of God. Then we are in a position to confess what God has already spoken in his word, and mixed with faith it will bring results. This will work in every area that we need to believe for, whether healing, guidance, protection, financial needs, or bringing up our children.

A DECEITFUL MOUTH

Proverbs 4:24 tells us to put away a deceitful mouth, and perverse lips. In other words, don't speak anything that is contrary to what the Word of God says. God calls that a deceitful and perverse mouth.

Many times parents speak negative words over their children, not realizing the effect that it has upon them.

"He'll never amount to much."

"She's a little demon!"

"You're wasting your time with him, he'll never change!"

These are all examples of a perverse and deceitful tongue, which the Bible says should be far from us.

OUT OF THE HEART

That is why it is so important to put God's Word in our heart first, because Matthew 12:34 tells us that out of the heart the mouth speaks. Eventually what is in our heart will come out. As we put God's Word in our heart concerning our children we will speak them out in faith, because faith will grow if we put His Word in our hearts.

HOLD FAST TO SOUND WORDS

"Hold fast the pattern of sound words, which you have heard from me, in faith and love which are in Christ Jesus."
2 Timothy 1:13

We are told to keep hold of sound words. This means speaking the promises of God over our children and holding fast to what He says, no matter what the situation looks like. When difficulties come and things look as though they are going backwards, instead of forwards, we have to keep hold of those sound words. God's sound words! We have to make sure we keep speaking them, and do not allow anything different to come out of our mouth.

Our words have power. Proverbs 18:21 tells us that life and death are in the power of the tongue, and you will eat the fruit of it. Somebody once said that sound words are like engines in your life. They start you off. They rev you up. They keep you running perfectly. I like that! God's Word gets you started. It shows you His will and His promises. It keeps you going through difficult circumstances and keeps you running the race until you're through.

MOUTH IN GEAR

So we need to get our mouth in gear, God's gear, if we want His results. We need to speak His Words boldly because the truth will set us free.

In Hebrews we are told that Jesus is the High Priest of our confession, and He is watching over our words to perform them. If we speak nothing, He has nothing to work with. If we speak a little, He has a little to work with. If we boldly speak a lot of His Word, guess what, He can actually work a lot on our behalf. Isn't it amazing that we can limit the work of God by what we don't say.

HELP YOUR CHILDREN WITH THEIR CONFESSION

When our children were small we would have fun with them confessing God's promises. I remember walking through woods on a family holiday. Their little legs were getting tired. As we helped them along we began to say, "I can do all things through Christ which strengthens me." We all began to march in time as we quoted this verse. Then Sean would quote the first part of the verse, "I can do all things..." and he would point suddenly to one of the children, and they would have to complete the verse. We were soon out of the woods, and the children had a word in their hearts that they would remember for the rest of their lives.

How many people even in old age can remember all the funny little nursery rhymes they learned as children. A child's mind absorbs so much in their formative years. Take the opportunities in every day life to confess God's word with them. It will make such a difference, and they will remember them for the rest of their lives.

"This is the day that the Lord has made. I will rejoice and be glad in it." We would remind ourselves, and our children, regularly with this scripture that whatever kind of day it was, we were going to rejoice and be glad in it, because it was the day the Lord had made. By doing that we were making a decision to obey God's word, and they were learning to rejoice in all situations.

THE TRANSFORMING POWER OF CONFESSION

Learning about the power of our confession transformed our lives as a family. We realized that we no longer had to put up with everything that came our way. On days when one of the family was not feeling well we began to say,
"By His wounds I have been healed."
"No weapon formed against me shall prosper."
"Jesus came that I might have life, and have it to the full."
"I am strong in the Lord and in His mighty power."

Then we began to say these confessions on good days, and we found that we didn't have nearly as many sick days as previously.

We were seeing before our eyes that our words have power. Proverbs tells us that life and death are in the power of the tongue and we will eat the fruit of it. We were beginning to experience that as we spoke God's healing promises we were becoming healthier. Those frequent visits to the doctor were now decreasing.

For several years one of our children had been seriously troubled with asthma. This meant endless trips to the doctor, weeks off school at a time and being rushed by ambulance to hospital to get her breathing under control. At that time in our lives we were just learning about the power of your confession. We began to speak healing scriptures over her. At the age of nine years old she began to get a hold of those scriptures for herself. She would walk around the house declaring the healing power of God over her life. Then she made a tape of the scriptures about healing. Next she got a notebook and wrote them down. At such a young age she was applying the Word of God to her life, giving it attention and filling her heart with it. She never had another attack. We saw the power of God in our own lives through confessing His promises.

IT'S NOT DIFFICULT

We were framing their world with the Word of God and encouraging our children to do the same. It's not difficult to do. Anyone can do it. You can begin today to start to frame your children's world with the Word of God.

This was what happened to Gideon when the Angel of the Lord

called him a mighty man of valour, in Judges 6:12. Gideon, at that time belonged to the weakest clan and he was the youngest in his father's house. He did not feel at all strong and mighty. But God was calling things that are not as though they were. (Romans 4:17) He was calling Gideon mighty, and Gideon went from being the weakest and the least to leading the Israelites into great victory. He was responsible for subduing the Midianites, who were their enemies, and bringing peace to Israel for forty years.

VICTORY SCRIPTURES

I once met a man who had great revelation about the power of confession. Every time he greeted us whether on the telephone or in person he would say, "Hello, you mighty woman of God, you overcomer, you victorious child of the King." Well I can tell you whatever I was dealing with that day I felt a whole lot better after talking to Him. I would be left thinking, "Yes I'm an overcomer, someone believes in me."

I started to confess these scripture over my children. Each day when they left for school I would call them a mighty man or woman of God, anointed by the Holy Spirit, empowered to prosper with the favour of God on them.

So I want to encourage you today to start to frame your children's world with the word of God. You will look back and be so glad that you did when you see the fruit of it in their lives.

SO SHALL MY WORD BE

> "For as the rain comes down, and the snow from heaven, And do not return there, but water the earth, and make it bring forth and bud, that it may give seed to the sower and bread to the eater, So shall my Word be that goes forth from my mouth: It shall not return to Me void, but it shall accomplish what I please, And it shall prosper in the thing for which I sent it."
> Isaiah 55:10-11

As I flew over Ireland recently I looked down at hundreds of fields all different, in shape, colour and size. It reminded me of God's Word. Why? In Ireland we experience a lot of rain. We call it the soft Irish rain, which basically means it is often damp! Because of this heavy rainfall the whole country has been known as the Emerald Isle. The rain has made it greener than most European countries. You see rain always has an effect. Whatever your country is like, when there is a rainfall it causes life and growth. Buds and shoots that have been lying dormant begin to appear.

The Bible says the Word of God is like that. His Word was never meant to be kept on the pages of a book, but on the hearts and mouths of His people. As you speak His Word over your children, life and growth begin to appear. Areas of their lives will begin to bud and flourish of which you may have been totally unaware. Gifts, dreams, and talents that have been lying dormant begin to come to life, because of the Word, which God likens to the rain. It is impossible for the Word to continually go out over our children and return void. God says it shall prosper and bring forth fruit, just like rain does to the countryside.

As you speak out God's promises for your children, understand that no Word of God is void of power. It must accomplish what he sent it to do. It will bring the impossible into the realm of the possible. As you speak out His Word over your children it will cause faith to rise in their hearts because faith comes by hearing and hearing by the word of God. As you frame their world with the Word of God their hearing will be fine tuned to what God says. They will have strong faith and be able to arise to be all that God has said. Don't make it difficult for your children by negative speaking but make a quality decision today to frame their young impressionable lives with faith filled words of life and power.

CHAPTER TEN

YOUR PRAYERS MAKE DYNAMITE AVAILABLE

"The earnest (heartfelt, continued) prayer of a righteous man, makes tremendous power available (dynamic in it's working)"
James 5:16 Amp

When you are right with God and walking in obedience, the Bible says your earnest prayer is powerful. It's not just any prayer from anyone. It is the prayer of someone walking in obedience and fellowship with God. It is not just any old casual prayer. It is the earnest, heartfelt, continuous prayer that works. There is nothing more earnest or heartfelt than the prayer of a parent for their child. They want the best for them and they want to see them have more opportunity then they did growing up. This heartfelt prayer makes tremendous power available not only for your child, but for thousands of others God wants to touch through you and your children. What a wonderful position to be in, to make tremendous power available. This power is like dynamite. It is full of energy and active. It gets things changed, opens doors of opportunity and blows obstacles out of the way. Parents you need to believe in your prayers. They make much power available on your children's behalf.

Many of the mighty men and women of God we see being used greatly had mothers who prayed and made power available. One such mother was Suzanne Wesley. She was the mother of John and Charles. They preached the gospel throughout Britain and Ireland causing great revival. Although she had seventeen children, she found the time to pray. Apparently she put her apron over her head each day and her children knew she was praying and not to be disturbed. Think of how many thousands of lives were saved through the ministry of her sons, for whom she prayed regularly. I believe that long after she had gone to be with the Lord, her prayers were still making dynamic power available for the lives of men and women on earth.

MY GRANDFATHER

I have heard stories of my grandfather, although I never met him, because he died before I was born. He apparently read the Bible every day to his children. He worked long hours in his bakery. But when he was not baking and delivering bread he would be found helping and visiting people or he would be found in the church. He was a man who loved God. I believe his prayers affected my life. God is no respecter of persons. His prayers are still at work on the earth making much power available. So be encouraged when you pray for your children and for others, for none of us know how far our prayers will reach but we do know that God will be faithful and he will make Holy Ghost, dynamic power available on our behalf.

BE A MOUNTAIN MOVER

"So Jesus answered and said to them, "have faith in God. For assuredly I say to you, whoever says to this mountain. Be removed and cast into the sea and does not doubt in his heart but believes that those things which he says will be done, he will have whatever he says. Therefore I say to you whatever things you ask when you pray, believe that you receive them and you will have them." Mark 11:22-24

Here Jesus is expecting his disciples to move obstacles and hindrances out of the way. They are to move them by speaking. They are to address the problem and command it to move then they are to believe in their hearts what they have said. Jesus tells them ask, believe and receive and they will have the answer. He says the same thing to us today. We are to ask and to believe that we receive and we will have the answer. As we pray for our children, we have the authority to speak to those mountains and difficult situations and command them to move. Jesus expects it of us. As your children hear you pray they will see answers and it will bring a sensitivity to them. Spend time praying with them and let them pray over issues. It is so encouraging for them to see that God answers their prayers. Help them to have a foundation of the Word of God and always have one or two scriptures that they are standing on.

In praying there are two key factors to having our prayers answered, found in John 15:7;

"If you abide in me and my words abide in you, you shall ask whatever you desire and it shall be done for you."

1.) Abiding, staying in fellowship.

2.) His word in us.

These are really the conditions God lays down for us. He then gives us an amazing promise. "You will ask what you desire and it will be done for you." There are really no limits to the power of our prayers if we will keep the conditions. We need to make sure that once we've asked we continually thank God for the answer. What you are continually thanking God for is what you will receive.

YOUR PRAYERS MAKE DYNAMITE AVAILABLE

When one of our children was small, she desperately wanted a bicycle. It was summertime and all the children were out on their bikes. We were not in a position to buy one at the time so I sat down and we prayed together, asked God for a bike. A few days later she came to me in tears - other children were out on their bikes and she had none. I reminded her that we had asked for a bike and we thanked God for it. One day a couple came to us and said "We have a bike for one of your children." We knew immediately which one, and when they told us, it was the one we had been praying with and thanking God for the answer. There is a great key here, in believing you receive when you pray and then holding fast to your confession until the answer is manifest. Remember, what you continually thank God for is what you will receive. He wants to give you the desire of your heart. Home is where our children should learn to pray. They learn by being with you when you pray, seeing you praying in the Holy Spirit. You are your children's best example. Show them how to pray, praise and pray until the answer comes.

"But beloved build yourselves up in the most holy faith praying in the Holy Spirit". Jude 20.

Train your children to pray in the Holy Spirit. From a young age they can do this with you, obviously they are not going to have the concentration span of an adult, but get them to pray loud enough to hear themselves. You pray with them. Have prayer times where they participate, share a scripture, lay hands on you and pray for you. In other words, include them. They will begin to love it. They will see God move in their lives.

Spiritual training begins at home not in Sunday school or Christian school. It must come first from home. Parents must take the responsibility for praying with their children. We have had many wonderful times with out children praying early in the morning, or after dinner at night. At first they didn't want to pray, but as we were persistent, and kept time short in the beginning, they began to enter in and eventually wanted to pray and would come and ask when are we going to pray "Can we get up early again tomorrow and pray together?" They could see it was changing their lives. So don't give up. Be persistent as you pray and include your children. You will make dynamic, Holy Ghost power available, and long after you and I have to be with the Lord our prayers will still be working on the earth.

NEGATIVE SPEAKING CAN NULLIFY PRAYER

Sometimes people pray for their children and then run around speaking negatively about their faults. They have just nullified their own prayers. If parents do not take time to love, encourage and discipline their children, they are not taking their God given responsibility to train them, and so they nullify their own prayers. Parents need to make sure that they do not mistreat the gift God has entrusted to them. I once knew someone who would run to every person in town to get them to pray for her children. She was always out drinking coffee and gossiping, she would never stay home and take responsibility. It had disastrous consequences for her children.

All the amount of praying in the world will not take the place of parents taking their responsibility to love, train, discipline and spend time with their children. All these principles work together and dove tail to produce the fruit that God requires.

We need to make sure we are obedient in everything that God requires for bringing up our children. It may seem quite a challenge, but God has equipped you with His Word and the Holy Spirit. He has given you the opportunity to pray and make dynamic power available. If you do it His way, you will not fail. Believe what he says about your prayers, that they really are making much power available, they really are bringing the power of God on the situation. Through you praying, dynamic, Holy Ghost power is made available on the earth.

CHAPTER ELEVEN

HOLY SPIRIT WISDOM

DECISIONS, DECISIONS AND MORE DECISIONS

Throughout our lives there are situations and circumstances with which to deal. Sometimes we do not know which way to go and what decisions to make. This can be particularly so when bringing up our children.

Our decisions are going to have consequences. In fact everything we are today is a result of decisions we have made. Decisions like, where shall I work? Who shall I marry? How will I serve God in the local church? What types of friends do I choose? What influences do I allow into my life? How do I teach and train my children? To what school should I send them? In all these areas we need the wisdom of God, and it is vital that we walk in his wisdom, because what we decide now will effect our future. But the wonderful news is this,

"In Christ are hidden all the treasures of wisdom and knowledge." Colossians 2:3

Which means if you are a believer you belong to Christ and he belongs to you and all wisdom and knowledge you need is found in him. The Amplified Bible explains it even better.

"In him all the treasures of (divine) wisdom comprehensive insight into the ways and purposes of God and (all the riches of spiritual) knowledge and enlightenment are stored and lie hidden." Colossians 2:3 Amp

This is really a wonderful key to have. That God has hidden for you, (not from you) the ways and purposes of God for you and your children. But how do I find this wisdom in my everyday situations? You may well ask.

Firstly you must have a close relationship with God, a hearing and teachable heart, able to take correction and to submit to authority.

Secondly you must be willing to listen to wise counsellors, Proverbs 15:22 tells us "without counsel the plans go awry, but in a multitude of counsellors they are established."

Thirdly be careful with whom you spend your time. "He who walks with the wise is wise, a companion of fools will be destroyed." Proverbs 13:20

THE WISE VERSES THE FOOL

The book of Proverbs presents two categories of people, the wise and prudent and the fool or mocker. The wise person seeks after wisdom, loves instruction and receives correction. The fool neglects discipline, is lazy, deceitful, he has a mocking attitude and will not receive correction. Each one is characterized by his response to parental and other authority. The wise person brings joy and delight and the fool brings disgrace, strife, and sadness. Proverbs encourages the reader to become wise and despises the fool in his folly.

Lets seek after wisdom, let's be honest with ourselves and with God and see if there are areas in which we are behaving more like a fool than a wise person. We need to be alert to line up our attitudes with the word of God.

WHAT IS WISDOM?

Wisdom is having a deep understanding of the ways and purposes of God. When we walk in wisdom our path is clear and open, not confused and complicated.

> **"Wisdom is the principle thing. Therefore get wisdom and in all your getting get understanding. Exalt her and she will promote you. She will bring you honour when you embrace her. She will place on your head an ornament of grace, a crown of glory, she will deliver you. Hear my son and receive my sayings, and the years of your life will be many. I have taught you in the way of wisdom I have led you in the right paths. When you walk your steps will not be hindered. When you run you will not stumble. Take firm hold of instruction. Do not let her go. Keep her for she is life." Proverbs 4:7-13**

This scripture is telling us to prize and value wisdom. It is the principle thing and though it costs you everything, you need to get wisdom and understanding, you need to prioritize the activities in your life to seek after it. If you don't prize and value it you won't go after it and you will let it go. So above all, prize wisdom and understanding and go after it so you can walk in it and receive the blessing.

ASK...He gives to all liberally. In order to get wisdom not only do we need to walk closely with the Lord and receive Godly counsel but also James 1:5 tells us to ask God who gives to everyone liberally without finding fault and it will be given. The one condition is that we ask in faith and do not allow doubt in otherwise we are unable to receive anything from the Lord.

Whatever situation you are in, whatever decision you need to make, identify the problem and then look for the answer or solution.

Answers will not come unless you look for them, and you will never find them while you focus on the problem. While you are looking for the solution think through and perhaps make a list of possibilities. Ask God to give you wisdom and believe you have received it. Do not forget He promises to lead and guide you into all truth. And as a righteous person, your steps are ordered by the Lord. As his sheep you hear his voice, so be confident in receiving God's wisdom. You will have peace in your heart about the way you should go, let that peace rule and reign in your heart.

THEN IT WILL BE TIME TO MAKE YOUR DECISION

Once you've made your decision you must follow it through with action to bring it to pass. By yielding to the Holy Spirit he will open up the scriptures to you about how to live your life in a way that pleases God. That is the purpose in asking for wisdom so we can fully please the Lord and enjoy the full fruit of it in our lives.

As you make the wisdom of God a priority in your life the Holy Spirit will work with you and show you things ahead of time and give you insight, understanding and discernment. Paul puts it so eloquently, in Colossians 1:9-12 summing up the benefits and blessings of walking in this wisdom.

"For this reason we also, since the day we heard it do not cease to pray for you and to ask that you may be filled with the knowledge of his will in all wisdom and spiritual understanding that you may walk worthy of the Lord, fully pleasing him, being fruitful in every good work and increasing in the knowledge of God." Colossians 1:9-12

That's God's will for you, that his wisdom will cause you to walk worthy of the Lord in bringing up your children and that will, in turn be fruitful. You will be strengthened supernaturally and have patience and long-suffering and a thankful heart because God has made you competent and qualified to partake of the inheritance that belongs to you. Part of that inheritance is having the wisdom of God to raise your children and to watch them become mighty in the land.

CHAPTER TWELVE

BUILDING CLOSE RELATIONSHIPS

Throughout the chapters of this book I have endeavoured to weave the importance of building close relationships with our children. It is so important that I feel it is worth looking at in closer detail.

The pace of life at the beginning of the new millennium is faster than it has ever been. Mothers work outside the home due to financial pressures and better career opportunities. Many demands are placed on fathers through business and work. Then there is the need for exercise and leisure time. Many Christians are quite rightly involved in serving in the local church. Life can be extremely challenging and fast moving. Among all these demands is the need to give quality time to our children. Even with busy schedules if the time we give is quality it makes up for some of the time when we are away.

It is a well-known fact that children today are suffering from neglect. When children are small they need parents there to be involved with them. A few minutes sitting on the floor building those blocks, and being intently involved in their world means so much. Reading with them at night before they go to sleep and taking time to say good night to them should be a priority. Look on it as a very important appointment, if somebody phones or calls to see you then you are unavailable until you have finished your appointment. You can always call them back and talk to them later, but guard those moments with your children or they will be stolen surreptitiously from you and you won't even know it.

This was brought home to me recently when a pastor shared how he had planned to spend some time with his children. It had been a busy season and he knew he needed time with the kids. They arranged for Saturday morning and planned to take some time out together. Late Friday night a phone call came from a distressed man with lots of problems. He had been to church a couple of times but they didn't really know him. The Pastor felt obliged to cancel the trip with his children and arranged an appointment with him instead. They talked for hours and although he was already a Christian he knew he needed to make some serious changes in his life. He would be in church on Sunday and start to get committed so that he could get built up in the Word of God and get his way of thinking renewed.

It seemed like a very successful time. However Sunday came and went, the Bible studies also came and went but the man with the problems was nowhere to be seen. Still carrying on in his old way of thinking and still holding on to his problems he was unwilling to change. And the children had been deprived from time with their father. He vowed never to let that happen again. Those of us in ministry need to guard against the situations that would steal time with our children. There will always be problems to solve, people to visit and sermons to preach, but we need to guard time with our families and treat it with utmost importance.

As they grow older we build relationships by talking and listening. Sometimes as parents we get used to giving instructions and need to listen as well. Communication is a two-way thing. We need to make sure we're not always instructing, but we're open to listen. And listening means full attention. I know that sometimes my children have said, Mum, you're not really listening! I may have been there in body, but my mind had wandered to something extremely important. They are not fooled. They soon get to know when you are preoccupied, so make sure you give them time when they have your full attention.

LOVE IS SPELT "T. I. M. E."

It is one thing to tell our children that we love them, and we need to do that regularly but if we really love them we will spend time with them. Find out what interests them, what likes and dislikes they have. You'll be amazed as they grow into teenage life they do actually have opinions. So be there to listen to them. When you give them the love and attention they need they are far less likely to run around looking for attention elsewhere.

Find things to do with them that they would like. Whatever it takes on your part as a parent work at building and keeping close relationships. This will be a strength when other situations present difficulties. Home relationships that are secure help our growing children to be stable and to function better in life as well as feel good about themselves.

HELPING THEM THROUGH DIFFICULTIES

Sometimes in life there will be difficulties for our children to handle, and we need to be aware of that and help them through it. We had a situation like that a while ago when one of our daughters had some guinea pigs, which she just adored. She would bath them and comb their long hair and take full responsibility for cleaning them out and feeding them. When Sean returned home from work one day he found that someone had been into our garden taken them out of the hutch and killed them. They both lay dead on the path. For our daughter who was about nine years old at the time this would be such a catastrophe, especially as the female was pregnant and she was excitedly waiting for the babies to be born. Sean phoned me and suggested that I leave work earlier to be at home to explain what had happened. I'm so glad I did. For her they were the most important part of her life after her immediate family. Being there to help her through it made all the difference.

OVER BUSY - OVER PREOCCUPIED

There are results that take place in a child's life when parents are over busy. Communication and trust begin to break down, opening the door to disappointment, depression and rebellion. When we as parents don't make time to see that our children complete a task properly and praise them for it, we can leave them feeling that in life, they can get by with anything. They will have no desire to do things well and achieve. Proverbs tells us that hope deferred makes the heart sick. By spending time and building relationships, we bring hope into our children's lives. With out it they become easily discouraged and give up. Building a close relationship will show them that you take genuine interest in all they do and truly care for them the way you should.

Many years ago I was teaching in a school and I taught a young boy. I'll call him James. He was struggling badly with his schoolwork, had no confidence and no drive about anything. I soon learned that James' father had left home and had promised every Tuesday to pick him up from school. Tuesdays would come and go but his dad would never appear, not even telephoning to say why. This badly affected James causing disappointment after disappointment. By the time I met him he didn't want to try anything or believe anything. Hope deferred had made his heart sick.

Gradually the Holy Spirit showed me ways to reach into his life by the use of encouragement. Each morning I made it a priority to greet him warmly. Looking right into his eyes, and touching his arm I would tell him I was really pleased to see him. In the beginning he would stare at me blankly, but as time went on he would even manage a smile and begin a conversation. When it came to work time other students had written a page he had managed one line. I knew it had taken great effort and told him that I was so pleased with his first line that I couldn't wait to see the next. I told him he was to do another line as soon as possible and bring it to show me. Gradually James' work began to increase. Instead of being so far behind the other children of his age he began to catch up. His confidence was being restored because someone believed in him.

It wasn't long before James' countenance began to change. He began to smile, to work harder because someone believed in him. As his self-esteem was lifted higher his interaction with the other children became more apparent. His mother later wrote me a very moving letter, telling me how much he had changed since he had been in my class. He had become more relaxed, and had started to talk happily about school, and was even beginning to make friends and trust people again. If he could have one wish it would be that I could always be his teacher, he had told his mother. I knew it wasn't me that he needed, but anyone who would be sensitive enough to encourage, and show interest in him, particularly while his relationship with his father was failing so badly.

Our world is full of children like James and parents need to take their responsibility to be consistent and reliable with their children. Yet even with a family situation like James had, young children can be influenced and transformed if you invest some encouragement time into them.

Then there was Dennis, a young five year old with a head of thick blonde hair. When school was over he was taken care of by teachers until six o'clock. At half past six his mother would arrive to collect him. Dennis would be in school from eight o'clock in the morning till nearly seven o'clock in the evening and he was showing major signs of neglect in his behaviour. He was clumsy and awkward, wanting to please and often rushing to be the first finished which made his presentation horribly messy. He had a good heart but was often misunderstood and frequently in trouble with the teachers. This would cause frustration to surface and his anger regularly resulted in the attacking of other pupils.

I made it my prerogative to sit and talk with Dennis, telling him that I didn't want to see him getting in trouble so much and I believed in him and wished to help him. We made it into a game and when he finished a class without misbehaving I would encourage him and make sure to tell his mother of his positive achievement. As behaviour improved we extended the time that he was expected to behave until he could stay out of trouble for a whole day. Dennis was less of a threat to other children and the other teachers lost less hair over him. His mother began to visit me to speak of his improvement and overall happiness. This gave me the opportunity to share with her the importance of encouraging and motivating this active little boy.

Both these cases are examples of young children whose homes are disrupted by obvious causes. It was nothing for me to give a few minutes of undivided attention to them each day. How much the more if we take the time to build relationships. Find things that your children can do with you. This may take a bit of effort on your part.

The younger they are the easier it is but as they get older there are more distractions and of course they will become more independent as they adapt to adult life. When our children were young we took them swimming every Monday evening for an hour. They returned from the pool on wet, cold winter nights to enjoy a large bowl of homemade soup by the fire. These winter evenings have now become special memories to them as they remember the family times spent by the fire and moments of fun during dark and cold winters.

When one of our teenage daughters went through a difficult stage, I knew I needed to spend more time with her. There were many friends and school acquaintances looking for her attention and I knew not all of them would be a great influence. So every Saturday I would take her to different shopping centers. I didn't have a lot of money to spend but it was time together. We would go specifically to see the things she liked (I resisted the urge to go to the places that I liked). This was a time for me to be interested in her likes and dislikes. I'd ask her about the music she liked and the types of clothes she enjoyed wearing. We played her type of music in the car instead of mine. Spending those Saturdays together really brought us close. It broke down the barriers that the devil had tried to put between us.

With one of my other daughters we spend one day a week baking. At first, the idea was not popular with her and I had to work at it. At the end of the morning however, when she has a plate of chocolate buns or a delicious dessert for all the household she is delighted. This time together gives the opportunity for us to communicate and talk while we are busy. It doesn't seem like work, just fun.

There are endless ways to build close relationships with your children, without control or trying to make them act just like you. Invest time into them throughout the week. Taking them away on their own for a few days brings a unique closeness enabling you to get inside their world.

SIGNS OF REBELLION

To be successful at parenting you will need to detect signs of rebellion early. A disease cannot be effectively treated until it is detected. With rebellion, barriers go up, misunderstandings occur and soon children withdraw, especially if they are teenagers.

I believe pre-teen life is vitally important. If you will invest time then it is not as likely that they will rebel in later years because the time you have invested will have brought you close.

If you notice that your child is sullen or withdrawn, take some time with them. Determine to spend quality time giving their needs your attention. That doesn't mean that you over indulge them, and encourage them to behave however they like. It means that you are attempting to find their heart, to discover what is really going on in their mind and to help them with it.

Fathers, take time with your sons. Do something together that they would enjoy on a regular basis. Fishing, football, golf or swimming, whatever it may be that they enjoy, open your heart to it so that you can build, build, build relationship.

God expected us to do this. The Bible talks about fellowship, which is what develops relationship. In Deuteronomy 6:6-7, God expected parents to spend time with their children, in the house, travelling, getting up and going to bed. That is pretty often!

Mothers, take time with your daughters. Enjoy a growing relationship. Teach them to cook or do a makeover, or manicure nails. How about letting your daughter style your hair for a change. Take them out to a coffee shop, fashion show or movie theatre. Have a girl's day out. Let them show you clothes that they think you should wear.

Bring them to the gym, play some tennis and go walking or cycling together. Or simply sit on their bed and talk.

If you hang around them long enough and frequently, they will open up their hearts to you and share what's going on. This is what builds relationship.

In order to have strong families we need to take time to build effective relationship skills. Don't be over busy or preoccupied with your own life but prioritize time with your children. This is simply you taking up your rightful responsibility.

Put a stop to the neglect that our children are suffering from and determine that, as for me, I will build close relationships with my child.

CHAPTER THIRTEEN

THE LIMITS ARE OFF

AFFECTING CITIES AND NATIONS

> **"For you will spread abroad to the right hand and to the left and your offspring will possess the nations and make the desolate cities to be inhabited." Isaiah 54:3 Amp**

Let's remind ourselves that whatever God says is already settled in Heaven. Whatever He says He absolutely means. Here, He tells us that our descendants will possess nations. Not one, but many. In other words they will have a powerful effect on whole nations for the glory of God. Isaiah 54 also says that our descendants will make the desolate cities to be inhabited. There are many ruined cities in the world. They may have the latest architecture, wonderful buildings and infrastructure, but behind it is a place full of people who are empty and whose lives are in ruins.

God says our children will bring a major change and cause the life of God to flow where there were once ruins. This scripture is really talking about a powerful, move of God affecting cities and nations and bringing change to millions of lives. God is not just looking at your little family and mine. His vision is much larger. It encompasses the cities and the nations of the world. It encompasses the millions of people who inhabit them. We are talking here about the heart of God reaching the people that He created and loves. We are talking about a move of God bringing the Gospel across the earth and touching many lives. Bringing the glory of God, the healing and the love of Jesus where once there was deep darkness over the people.(Isaiah 60:2)

RAISE YOUR CHILDREN TO KNOW THEIR GOD

Our children need to develop their own relationship with God. We help them in their formative years, but then they are weaned from us and want to spend time with God for themselves. I was talking to my oldest daughter, Rebecca, recently about what makes one young person keep walking with God and another fall away. Her reply was, "Their own relationship with God, praying in the Holy Spirit, and spending time with Him."

That is so true. When we develop our own relationship with God our trust in Him grows stronger and we become more secure as people. Our children can know there is someone to turn to in any situation. Who has plans to prosper them and not to harm them, plans to give them a great future. The Bible says the people who know their God will be strong and carry out great exploits - Daniel 11:32. That is the key to the limits being taken off. Our children need to know God for themselves. This will make them strong and they will achieve great victories because of the great God they know working in them and through them.

EXAMPLES FROM THE BIBLE

There are many examples from the Bible of children and young people who had a great influence on lives for God. A little servant girl suggested to her mistress that Naaman the leper should go to see the prophet of God and he would be healed. The story can be found in 2 Kings 5. This little girl saved her master's life by telling her mistress that Naaman could be healed of his leprosy. She brought hope to a hopeless situation and lives were forever changed.

DAVID THE GIANT KILLER

Then there was the young shepherd boy David who knew his God. When he was out on the hills looking after the sheep, he would worship and sing to God. During that time his flock was attacked by a lion and a bear. On each occasion he took the lamb from their mouths and killed the predators. Although he was the one who dealt the fatal blow he knew it was God who had delivered him. So when he heard that Goliath the Philistine was challenging the Israelite army, he volunteered immediately to fight him. He was confident in the God who had delivered him from both the lion and the bear. In the natural he was not trained to be a soldier and was unskilled in using armour, but he ran towards the enemy. He was so sure of his God that he declared beforehand to the Philistine that on that very day he would take off his head and every one would know there was a God in Israel. And that is exactly what happened. You can read about it in 1 Samuel 17. David was a young man who knew his God and carried out great exploits.

THREE YOUNG MEN WHO WOULD NOT COMPROMISE

In Daniel 3, we read of three young men who refuse to compromise. They knew and loved God and even though there was a death threat to any one who would not bow down to the golden image of King Nebuchadnezzar, they still would not compromise. Shadrach, Meshach and Abednego declared to the King that God was able to deliver them from the fiery furnace that had been prepared. And even if He did not, they still would not bow down. Nebuchadnezzar was furious, the furnace was heated seven times hotter than usual. It was so hot that it killed the soldiers who took the young men and threw them into the flames. When the King looked into the furnace, He saw

Shadrach, Meshach and Abed-Nego, no longer tied but loosed and walking around. With them was a fourth man looking like the Son of God!

These were three young men who would not compromise. God miraculously delivered them and the King changed the Law because He saw their God was real. These are just some of the miracles that have happened because young people walked with God. The limits were removed, great victories accomplished and many lives impacted. God's will for our children is that they are mighty while they live on the earth. That does not mean they will not have battles and struggles and times of discouragement but it means they will know how to overcome, how to move on with God and how to go from strength to strength. This Holy Spirit move of God will affect many lives and bring the Good News across the earth into cities, towns and homes. It will touch the lives of ordinary people and bring them the love and healing power of Christ.

There is no limit to how God will use our children. As parents we need to get hold of what God has promised in his word, and set our faces like flint to raise up a powerful generation. As our children know their God, they will be strong and carry out great exploits. We can believe for them to do exceeding abundantly above all we could ask or think, and the limits will be taken off the move of God as it advances through the earth producing much fruit and bringing great glory to God.

CHAPTER FOURTEEN

THE REWARDS OF YOUR LABOUR

THE PROMISE OF REWARDS

Wherever you are right now concerning bringing up your children God has promised wonderful rewards. God is a God of purpose and destiny, and has a great purpose for your children. If they are still small, keep doing what you know to do, and trust God to do what you can't. In bringing up children there is your part and God's part. Be faithful to do your part, and God will be faithful to do His.

If they are older, and maybe away from the Lord, start standing on His promises for them to come back to the Lord.

It is important for you to know that your labour is not in vain in the Lord. All that training, disciplining, teaching and encouragement will bring forth a harvest, and will have great rewards. So stay encouraged, don't grow weary in being a parent. Believe in the faithfulness of God to do exceeding abundantly above all you could ask or think, according to the power that is at work within you.

JOY AND DELIGHT

> "The father of the righteous will greatly rejoice, And he who begets a wise child will delight in him."
> "Let your father and mother be glad, and let her who bore you rejoice." Proverbs 23:24-25

Children who are walking uprightly before God will bring a great amount of joy to their parents. A child who is wise, handling life's situations with the wisdom of God will bring great delight to his parents, and will be the means of causing blessing and rejoicing. Instead of being anxious and concerned, you can be at peace and rest, knowing that your child has grown up to be wise, making good decisions with integrity and honour.

That is the kind of person God promises to exalt and honour. In Deuteronomy 28:1-14 we find a list of the blessings that God promises to overtake those who walk in obedience to Him. What a powerful amount of blessings to overtake both you and your children as you earnestly follow Him.

MY HEART WILL REJOICE

"My son, if your heart is wise, my heart will rejoice indeed, I myself; Yes, my inmost being will rejoice when your lips speak right things." Proverbs 23:15-16

When your children walk with the Lord speaking truthfully and honestly, it is a great reward. It should cause parents to have a cheerful heart, which in turn will be like good medicine to them, and do them good.

Proverbs 15:20 Describes a wise son as bringing joy to his father. Every wise son should have respect and honour for his parents. The Holy Spirit can heal any difficulties there have been between children and parents bringing them into a wonderful relationship that brings great joy.

In Proverbs 31:28, we read that children will arise and call their mother blessed. She has been a virtuous woman, and now her children are declaring good things over her life. They are rising up and blessing her. What a beautiful reward to be blessed by the ones that you have sacrificed for and put so much into.

PEACEFUL CHILDREN

When your children live in peace, it brings great blessing to them and to you. Peace in their lives means nothing missing, nothing broken, no fear or dread, nothing to torment them, but living in the very presence and blessing of God. This is what Isaiah 54:13 says

"All your sons shall be taught by the Lord and great shall be their peace."

Expect that peace in their lives and it will alone be a wonderful reward for you. You won't have to worry or think twice about where they are or what they're up to, knowing they walk with the Lord will bring great peace.

"Behold children are a heritage from the Lord. The fruit of the womb is a reward like arrows in the hand of a warrior so are the children of ones youth. Happy is a man who has his quiver full of them. They shall not be ashamed. But shall speak with their enemies in the gate." Psalm 127:3-5

Children are a wonderful reward from the Lord. Verse 5 of Psalm 127 tells us that they will even contend with our enemies. They will bring strength to our lives and be strong against things that have been enemies to us.

Our children belong to God. They're ours only in the sense to bring up and train. God has entrusted us with an amazing responsibility and opportunity.

As we teach and train them in the way they should go, God promised they will not depart from it. He promises us the blessings and rewards of wise children who love and walk with him. At the end of it we will be able to say, it was worth it - God has been so faithful. It brings us back to the picture we talked about in the first chapter of this book. The picture of God's will for our children being full of the Holy Spirit, affecting cities and nations, focused and strong in the Land, and walking closely with Him, being anointed and greatly used by God.

What a wonderful reward - Great peace and joy as parents - and to be able to see it with our own eyes; exactly as God said it would be - My children are truly mighty in the land.

SALVATION

For those who don't know Jesus but would like to:

Dear Lord, through the principles of your word in the pages of this book, I have been challenged to change. Right now I declare Jesus Christ as the Lord and Saviour of my life. I confess that I have sinned and made many unwise decisions that need to be washed away by the blood of Jesus today.

I now determine to adhere to those principles of wisdom, love and faith, which you have so faithfully compiled for me in your word. I am not ashamed to be called a Christian but will daily be involved in prayer and Bible-reading and weekly be involved in church fellowship.

Thank you Father for restoring my joy and my peace and giving me the desire to follow your commands wholeheartedly.
In Jesus' name, Amen.

CONFESSIONS OF A PARENT

I thank you Lord that because I fear you and delight greatly in your commands my children will be mighty in the Land. (Psalms 112:2 NIV)

Because my children honour and obey their parents things go well for them and they have long life. (Ephesians 6:2)

They dwell in the secret place of the Most High.
God is their refuge and fortress.
No evil shall befall them, no plague shall come near them.
You are with them Lord, in times of trouble.
You deliver them and honour them.
You satisfy them with long life and show them your salvation.
They walk under the shadow of your wings. (Psalms 91)

Your blessing is upon them and they grow up declaring boldly that they belong to You, You are their God. (Isaiah 44:2-5)

My children keep your commands, mercy and truth are in their hearts and they find favour and high esteem with God and man.

They trust you with all their heart, therefore you direct their path. (Proverbs 3:1-6) They will walk with the wise and therefore they are wise. They do not hang around ungodly people but delight in your law and meditate in it day and night. Whatsoever they do prospers. (Psalm 1:2-3)

No weapon formed against them will prosper and no tongue raised against them shall stand.
(Isaiah 54:17)

They know their God and therefore they are strong and carry out exploits. (Daniel 11:32)

They are God's workmanship and walk in the good paths that God has prepared beforehand for them. (Ephesians 2:10)

They are overcomers, they overcome by the blood of the lamb and the word of their testimony. (Revelation 12:11)

They are faithful and abound with blessings. (Proverbs 20:20)

They are blessed in the city and blessed in the country. (Deuteronomy 28:3)

They increase more and more.
They are blessed coming in and blessed going out.
You command a blessing upon my children.
You open the good treasure of the heavens to bless all the works of their hands.
They are lenders not borrowers.
They are the head and not the tail.
They are above and not beneath. (Deuteronomy 28:1-14)

You surround them with favour as with a shield. Your favour is upon them. (Psalms 5:12)

The spirit of increase is upon my seed, and they increase more and more. (Psalms 115:14)

By your wounds they have been healed and walk in divine health. (Isaiah 53:2-5)

You are the strength of their life and their portion forever (Psalms 73:26)

Because they seek after wisdom and understanding, they have promotion and honour. Grace and Glory are upon them. (Proverbs 4:6-9)

As tithers, the windows of heaven are open over their lives and blessing is poured out upon them. (Deuteronomy 28:12)

The blessing of the Lord makes them rich and adds no sorrow. (Proverbs 10:22)

They are empowered to prosper and so establish God's covenant in the earth. (Deuteronomy 8:18)

Father God, You said that if I favour your righteous cause you would take pleasure in prospering my children, so I stand now on my covenant with you knowing that you shall prosper my children. (Psalms 35:27)

You have wonderful plans for my children to prosper them and not to harm them to give them a future and a hope. Let the plans unfold NOW! (Jeremiah 29:11)

God's mercies are new every morning over my children, His compassions do not fail them because of His great love. Great is His faithfulness to them. (Lamentations 3:23)

I refuse to raise lazy, idle, apathetic men to serve in God's kingdom. My sons will be "Psalms 119" type men. They will be successful, loving, compassionate and faithful. They will be clean living, hard workers who lead their families into success. (Psalms 119:9)

I refuse to raise sarcastic, insecure, proud or spoilt daughters in my home. My daughters shall be "Proverbs 31" type girls. They shall be virtuous, honourable, discrete and holy. They shall be servant hearted prayer warriors, always ready to willingly lend a hand with out thought of reward. (Proverbs 31:10-31)

(Psalms 112:2)
All of my children shall be taught of the Lord.
All of my children shall have great peace.
I will not settle for any less, for right now I take my God-given responsibility to take authority over every wicked force that seeks to have my children. I serve the devil my covenant contract now:

"ALL MY CHILDREN SHALL BE MIGHTY IN THE LAND IN JESUS MIGHTY NAME" AMEN!